ADVANCE PRAISE FOR

Receiving God and Responding, in Breath Meditation

"Drawing on traditional Christian teaching from the first century to the present about the Holy Spirit as the Breath of God, Joseph Piccione offers us a way of contemplative prayer that is both simple and profound. Breathing attentively in the way he describes allows us not only to rest in a wordless awareness of being God's Beloved but also prompts or "nudges" us toward a caring love for all our brothers and sisters – a truly integrated spirituality."
—Abbot James Wiseman, O.S.B., Saint Anselm Abbey, Washington, D.C.; Editor and translator, *John Ruusbroec: The Spiritual Espousals and Other Works*

"The Apostle Paul enjoins Christians to 'pray without ceasing' (1 Thess 5:17). This book lays out concrete guidelines by which this can be realized in our daily lives, and opens us to new horizons in experiencing God's loving presence in our midst."
—Ruben L.F. Habito, Professor of World Religions and Spiritual Formation, Perkins School of Theology, Southern Methodist University; Author of *Living Zen, Loving God* and *Healing Breath: Zen for Christians and Buddhists in a Wounded World*

"This interesting and erudite work focuses on the connection between breath and spirit in Christian spirituality. Breath is something we receive as a gift. Piccione makes the point, backed up by a wide range of references, that our relationship with God is, like the breath on which we depend, primarily receptive. As he puts it, "Breathing becomes receiving." So, to grow spiritually, we need to learn how to "breathe with receptivity.""
—Louis Hughes, O.P.
Author of *The Art of Allowing: The Breath in Meditation and in Life*

Receiving God and Responding, in Breath Meditation

Receiving God and Responding, in Breath Meditation

Praying at the Intersection of Christian Trinitarian Spirituality and the Breath Practice of Zen and Mindfulness

JOSEPH J. PICCIONE

A HERDER & HERDER BOOK
THE CROSSROAD PUBLISHING COMPANY
NEW YORK

A Herder & Herder Book
The Crossroad Publishing Company www.crossroadpublishing.com

© 2020 by Joseph J. Piccione

Crossroad, Herder & Herder, and the crossed C logo/colophon are registered trademarks of The Crossroad Publishing Company.

All rights reserved. No part of this book may be copied, scanned, reproduced in any way, or stored in a retrieval system, or transmitted, in any form or by any means, electronic, mechanical, photocopying, recording, or otherwise, without the written permission of The Crossroad Publishing Company. For permission please write to rights@crossroadpublishing.com.

In continuation of our 200-year tradition of independent publishing, The Crossroad Publishing Company proudly offers a variety of books with strong, original voices and diverse perspectives. The viewpoints expressed in our books are not necessarily those of The Crossroad Publishing Company, any of its imprints or of its employees, executives, or owners. Although the author and publisher have made every effort to ensure that the information in this book was correct at press time, the author and publisher do not assume and hereby disclaim any liability to any party for any loss, damage, or disruption caused by errors or omissions, whether such errors or omissions result from negligence, accident, or any other cause. No claims are made or responsibility assumed for any health or other benefits.

The text of this book is set in 11/14 Sabon LT Pro.

Composition by Sophie Appel
Front cover image and cover design by Joseph J. Piccione
Back cover image by Andrei Rublev, The Trinity

Library of Congress Cataloging-in-Publication Data
available upon request from the Library of Congress.

ISBN 978-0-8245-9807-5 paperback
ISBN 978-0-8245-0180-8 cloth
ISBN 978-0-8245-0181-5 ePub
ISBN 978-0-8245-0182-2 mobi

Books published by The Crossroad Publishing Company may be purchased at special quantity discount rates for classes and institutional use. For information, please e-mail sales@crossroadpublishing.com.

CONTENTS

Acknowledgments	vii
Prayer within Faith and Life	1
Part I — Foundations for Practice	19
Chapter 1 — Breathe	21
Chapter 2 — Receive	29
Chapter 3 — Respond	51
Part II — Practice	59
Chapter 1 — Breathing	61
Chapter 2 — Receiving	73
Chapter 3 — Responding	83
Part III — Living with Ourselves and Others	103

Acknowledgments

M Y ACKNOWLEDGMENTS AND GRATITUDE to:

Our familial community of love. Beloved Nancy and our beloved children Francesca, Giuliana and Joseph. This book began in family conversations and Francesca's requests to "write this down for me." Thank you for your nudges.

And to an essential wider community. To spiritual leaders Ruben Habito and Fr. Louis Hughes, O.P. for their support. To Jon Magnuson and Ruth Almén for the circles of receptivity and meditation they created. In the Saint Mary's years, to Fr. Philip Keane, P.S.S. and Patricia Lamoureux, and in the Dominican years, to Fr. William Newman, O.P., Rev. Archimandrite Joseph Lee, and Fr. Thomas Heath, O.P. A particular thanks to Chris Myers of Herder and Herder for his welcome and encouragement.

Prayer within Faith and Life

THEOLOGY, IN ITS ANCIENT Christian understanding, was not so much an academic topic but an orientation for hearing and responding to God and entering into Trinitarian life as individuals in community. Orthodoxy, right teaching, was for orthopraxis, right practice, and relationship. Theological words are necessary, but not for their own sake.

Our study hopes to pick up this earlier theological method for awareness of the energy of Trinitarian life and activity and offer ways to enter into the loving dynamic of reception and response. We will propose a renewed Christian understanding of reception of the breath as a symbol of God's loving intimacy with us. We will offer a method to enter into a breath-based meditation as a foundation for prayer and contemplative living in an integrated spirituality inclusive of God Trinity, our sisters and brothers, and our sister Mother Earth.

Within the Christian tradition, humanity's relationship with God might be put simply and in a contemporary sense: Relationship with God happens by being human. God knew us in our uniqueness from eternity in Christ. Christ is disclosed as the Beloved, and humanity is disclosed as Beloved in the Beloved. It is simply who we are. Quite stunningly, we are related to God and thus related to everyone and everything; our personal reality is intimate and cosmic.

God's inner relationality is called Trinity and is Christianity's core teaching or doctrine. God Trinity is a personal, inner love relationality, and if we take that seriously, relationality with God and others is unavoidable. Reception and response is the heartbeat of Trinitarian life and for relationship in ourselves. Relationship involves presence and action. Action might be heavily emphasized at times, and thus it is essential to identify presence as foundational.

Meditation, as well as contemplative prayer and living, is a primary way to develop and maintain an abiding presence relationship in God Trinity's invitation to love.

It seems critical for Christianity at this moment in history to reclaim its identity as invitation to reception of relationship and responsive experience in prayer, and then to facilitate its practice. When our inward God Trinity relationship becomes the core understanding of prayer, a relational dynamic of receive and respond can begin.

Meditative prayer will deepen the love relationship in contemplative living, of course, and the gifts of the Holy Spirit move us to a state of freedom from bondage to any inhumane and self-centered aspects we find in ourselves, deepening our relationships of love for all persons. Mature freedom is expressed in personal consistency and fidelity.

Prayer awareness means finding ourselves within Trinitarian relationship and spirituality as manifold connections to Trinitarian life. Blessed John Ruusbroec was a fourteenth-century European contemplative and spiritual writer. He is very reliable, and his teachings have unique inflections with their own distinctive appeal. Blessed John's writings serve as an inspiration and a guide in this presentation of meditation.

Blessed John taught that God is not alone but is the Trinity of love, and God is not isolated but wholly intending a loving "reciprocal activity" in mutual contentment (a word he often used) with us. Reflection on God's active relational reciprocity will cause our "love and sense of contentment to be renewed."[1]

Reciprocity with God Trinity and contentment in relationship would seem revolutionary, but is treasured in Christianity's quiet and sometimes hidden contemplative tradition. The inward tradition is renewed in our everydayness.

This book and method intend to share the tradition, reaching back to Scripture and voices of Christian ancestors, as well as the intersection of meditation insights from the world's wisdom traditions. It is offered to persons who are perhaps seeking a new way to live a simple, presencing spirituality of reception and response in their Christian faith, as well as for persons who are somewhat established in their spiritual practice.

Prayer can be reimagined as loving awareness or active presencing within our Trinitarian relationship. Far from being static, it is a presence that has changing shapes. Prayer will entail words over our lifetime, as well as moving beyond words and concepts in experience.

Our contemporaries voice hope for a renewed approach to prayer and seek an opportunity to go beyond the limit of words in our prayer relationship. This study on prayer (Part I) and presentation of prayer practice (Part II) arises within our contemporary longing for encounter with God as a basis for living.

Sources for Our Method

Specific attention to "breath" and reliance on "breathing practice" within our Trinitarian, Christian theological experience is distinctive in our prayer theory and practice. Breathing within Christian spiritual awareness is both the symbol of reception and of response. It emerges within the ancient Christian prayer traditions of the Eastern and Western Churches and in intersectional dialogue with Asian spiritual and wisdom traditions.

Cultural intersectionality is a hallmark of Christian experience. St. Paul opened the door. Over the centuries, Christians have enculturated the Good News by affirming strengths of new cultures and learning through encounter. The use of Greek philosophy in formulating the creeds of the Church is an early example.

Encounters with Asian spirituality and thought now have a similar role. The unique contribution of Asian practice to this Christian prayer practice for contemplative living is Zen attention to the breath for enlightened awareness and our Christian rediscovery of God's accompaniment in the breath.

Scholars of Scripture have opened up the biblical lexicon, including the meaning of breath, over the course of the twentieth century. Yet I believe there was relatively little practical spiritual interest in the meaning and significance of "breath" for decades, until encounters with Asian spiritual practice in the latter part of the century. Asian encounters both contribute important practice elements and bring us back to the breath in Judeo-Christian anthropology and self-understanding, which is the basis of prayer. We relate to God and others based on our sense of them and ourselves.

During the twentieth century, Catholic monks in Asia and Jesuits in Japan immersed themselves in dialogue with Buddhist monks and in *koan* and breath-based practice to understand the culture. It was a time of mutual engagement that encouraged a return to exploration of the contemplative tradition in Christianity with insights gained from these encounters.

Irish Jesuit William Johnston was among the first to share his findings with the English-speaking world. He appreciated the availability of meditative practice at a time when the West was drifting toward ever more noise and endless activity. Johnston found more of a crisis of prayer than a crisis of belief in the West. He appreciated St. Thomas Aquinas equally as a mystic and a theologian, and engaged the East with the mystical tradition of the West.[2]

Buddhism has an inner sociological dimension similar to Christianity in that there are many branches with their own organizations and spiritual practices. Zen can be approached by some, including myself, more as a breath-based than *koan-* or thought-based meditation practice, which was the prime practice found in many mid-twentieth-century conversations with Buddhism. My encounter with Zen came in the writings of Vietnamese monk Thich Nhat Hanh.

Thich Nhat Hanh's practice pressed me to explore what breath might mean for Christian prayer if we took the meaning of breath seriously, beyond abstraction, to practice. At first, my hope was to foster recollection for my own traditional Western discursive meditation, the three steps of which are recollection; reflection on Scripture, the Gospel teachings of Christ, or a doctrine of the faith; and an integration of loving response to God.

Zen gave me a push in practice to envision that breathing can become the Spirit's intimacy for us in the moment. Zen practice seeks enlightened awareness in the moment, based on Buddhist teachings, or dharma. Zen practice brought me, as a Christian living according to Christian teaching, to a new awareness of the moment in the light and wisdom of the Holy Spirit—a Zen-like Christian awareness. My integration of insights from Thich Nhat Hanh's Zen practice gave me a great appreciation, indebtedness, and fondness for this spiritual master.

Thich Nhat Hanh helped me to revisit William Johnston's writings and note his support for breath-based meditation. When Johnston wrote *Christian Zen* in 1970, it seemed so foreign to the West. Decades later, the West was very ready for it, as the Mindfulness movement, based on Jon Kabat-Zinn's remarkable translation of Buddhist practice to a secular model in the United States, had opened breath practice to countless persons who use it for a range of purposes. Living for many years in the United States, Thich Nhat Hanh was able to use the new awareness of breath meditation for his presentation of appreciative awareness and compassion in the moment given to us.

This study and method arose in part from the new awareness of breath practice in twentieth-century Christian writers to support accessible meditation and contemplative living through encounter with Zen. Johnston, in particular, posed the question about breath practice: "I believe that a whole method of Christian prayer associated with the breathing could be developed. But perhaps the time for this has not yet arrived."[3] Now, however—given the greater awareness of the use of breathing practice—appears to be an opportune moment to return to Johnston's invitation.

Our study hopes to provide both the theological foundation and application in practice for a method of "Christian prayer associated with the breathing." Certainly, it hopes to spark focused discussion at a time when increasing numbers of Christians are in fact practicing Mindful breathing and are expressing renewed interest in Christian meditation and contemplative living.

Numerous Christian spiritual writers are now incorporating breathing awareness. These include Augustinian Martin Laird and James Finley, who devotes a chapter to it as a way to find recollection and peace as a preface to prayer.[4] Other Christian writers, such as Ruben Habito and Paul Knitter, have entered deeply into Buddhist and Christian spirituality and share understandings in a complementary manner.

In *The Healing Breath of Zen*, Habito insightfully writes that "Christian spirituality is literally a life led in the Spirit, or Breath, of Jesus Christ." He looks for everyday, concrete applications in Christian spirituality.[5] In *Without Buddha I Could Not Be a Christian*, Paul Knitter writes that the "heart and ongoing heartbeat of Christianity is a mystical union with the Christ-Spirit." He finds that the Sacrament of the Eucharist, or Lord's Supper, and the Sacrament of Silence, in a breath-based prayer, keeps this alive.[6]

A generation earlier, in the mid-twentieth century, Trappist Thomas Merton expanded contemplative prayer beyond the cloister walls, a remarkable achievement. Benedictine John Main developed the Centering Prayer method in the twentieth century. Widely practiced, it uses breath for recollection. We are fortunate to live in a vibrant era of explorations into our ancient meditative prayer traditions and the integration of spirituality as a basis for living.

Our study gathers insights from the Zen use of breath and incorporates it, in a specifically Christian application, as a practice open to all Christians. As a Christian prayer practice, our model is intentionally, distinctively, and deeply Trinitarian.

Meditation is both ancient and constantly rediscovered in Christianity. Contemporary scholarship has lent new life to forgotten texts and fostered appreciation of the great pluralism of Christian spiritual practices. Among contemporary authors, there are many examples of cultural and religious intersectionality. Centering Prayer uses a Christian mantra in a repeated manner, adapting the technique from Hindu and Buddhist use.

Irish Dominican Louis Hughes presents a strong Christian understanding of breath in a meditation framework adapted from yoga practice.[7] My intersectionality is close in spirit to Hughes, who uses an entirely Christian appreciation of breath and its symbolism, employing insights from yoga practice. This study brings the same Christian instinct to Zen practice.

In the course of my explorations, I realized that my Christian brothers and sisters might be surprised by the application. In fact, I was surprised myself by the turns it took. Good surprises can happen in careful, reflective intersectionality. At the same time, I would not be surprised if our ancient Christian ancestors or the medieval beguines followed the same path of living awareness of the intimacy of the Spirit that the reader will find here.[8] Perhaps this study is as much recovery as development.

As the Spirit is always one with the Word and the Father, our practice is intentionally Trinitarian. The inner dynamic of God's Trinitarian life of invitation-response is the template for our own reception-response dynamic of life in God Trinity. As Trinity encompasses everything in love, contemplative prayer is inclusive and unbounded in scope. As one enters deeply into Trinitarian awareness, one's love and sorrow for persons experiencing suffering and injustice expand unbounded. We are inwardly moved to love, justice, and reconciliation.

PRAYER WITHIN FAITH AND LIFE

Our approach is given energy by ancient Christian belief in the active presence of the Holy Spirit, grounded in the spirituality of the Christian East. Early in his comprehensive study, Tomas Spidlik identifies the experience of the Spirit, or mysticism of the heart, as a foundational characteristic:

> Aspirations towards a conscious experience of grace were not unknown in the ancient East.... Orthodox authors never dreamed of denying the transcendence of God and the mysterious nature of his presence in man. If vivid feelings are not the sole and infallible manifestation of the divine life in man, "they are nevertheless a sign of perfect spiritual health," noted Theophane the Recluse.[9]

Experience of the Spirit is not sought as an end or goal. Our movement of presencing love in response to the Trinity is the very life of meditation. But love is always prompted by God, even in our prayer. As our Christian ancestors teach us, a prayer and meditation method disposes us to God's actions and does not cause them.

The Spirit's action within us is very difficult to describe, but the fruits of the Spirit, particularly peace, joy, and love (Gal 5:22), were seen as broadcast gifts by St. Paul and are experienced by us, often very deeply. We are not accustomed to attention to the Spirit's movements, healing, consolations, and nudges. Our reluctance must be questioned. Why would Christians exclude the possibility or normalcy that the Spirit, who is love and prompts our love in prayer, would not console us with loving rest? Our hymns sing of the Spirit as consoler. Are we used to God being distant and remote? Early Christian confidence in the intimacy of God beckons us and may offer a path for more Christians in the future.

Further appreciation arises in the teaching and insights of Blessed John Ruusbroec, which nudged me from prayer largely relying on thoughts and words to a new balance with an apogee in imageless relational prayer. Blessed John's writings created the path for our method; his is the basis and foundation for my intersectionality with Thich Nhat Hanh. Blessed John is considered to be among the most illumined of Western Christian contemplatives.

Practical insights from Zen master Thich Nhat Hanh are priceless and abound here; I find them so complementary in the new practical model that follows. Influence deriving from the Orthodox hesychast monastics and their prayer of quiet and of the heart has also been formative and a sign of the recovery of shared common longing for God in the Christian East and West.

The widespread use of Mindfulness and its basis in breathing practice provides a certain ease for persons who wish to use our prayer method. If you, the reader, have Mindfulness experience, you are most welcome, and may already be advanced in foundational breath awareness.[10] My hope is that you would find in our method a deepening of your Christian prayer through openness to the work of the Holy Spirit and a new application in your breathing practice.

Breath prayer can become, as presented in this method, foundational to an integrated spirituality of reception and response to ourselves in self-remembering; to God Trinity; to our sisters and brothers and the world in which we live.

Christian breath practice, as I propose with the theological symbolism of the breath with the Holy Spirit, can place us in the here and now of the dynamic personal invitation-response of God to us in the moment. Carmelite mystic St. Elizabeth of the Trinity wrote that "each minute is given us in order to 'root' us deeper in God" and to "mark everything with the seal of love!"[11]

Thich Nhat Hanh often wrote that breath practice is our way of coming home to ourselves in the moment. Breath as physical phenomenon is available to us and renews without our awareness. It can renew in an integrated manner with the awareness of and reception to the Holy Spirit, the Breath of God. Enlightenment is the work of the Spirit with our collaboration. Once learned, it becomes so immediate and simple. I believe it can become a practice foundation for contemplative living.

Situating Prayer in Life and Life's Theology: Centrality of the Trinity in Historical Theological Reflection

Christian theological reflection on our life in God spans two millennia of conversation. This section begins with the insights of a critically important contemporary writer and weaver of earlier insights on the active proximity of God to humanity.

Jesuit theologian Karl Rahner's anthropology presents the human person as fundamentally oriented to and consummated in God. The Incarnation is God's self-bestowal to humanity in an irrevocable manner. In the gift of the Holy Spirit, God is forever immanent to humans. Rahner's expression "supernatural existential" means that our everydayness in this moment is within the divine sphere of God's immanent presence and self-bestowal unto the consummation of the world, despite the tragic contradictions of humanity and our history. The supernatural existential means that God is not extrinsic to humanity, and so quenching the transcendental would be to "evolve backwards." Rahner calls humanity God's project.

Rahner found spirituality to be both individual and living within the history and sacramentality of the unique churches. One of the most cited statements of Rahner is that "the Christian of the future will be a mystic or he will not exist at all." By mysticism he did not mean "singular parapsychological phenomena, but a genuine experience of God emerging from the very heart of our experience." An experience of God is effected by God; we can dispose ourselves to God. And Rahner notes the difficulty of relating an experience of God to other persons; we can only "stammer" about it.

Rahner recognized the singular importance of the person's relationality in God, as well as the opportunities to experience the presence and activity of God in group settings.[12] In an essay based on a 1977 lecture, he expressed his belief that a vibrant spirituality will emerge as increasingly important in the future; we see this in our own time as individuals seek a life-rooted and not abstract relationship to God or the transcendent.

Our model intends to present Christian prayer and life in God and in God with others in an applied Trinitarian manner, trying, for the sake of manageable length, to use a minimal suitable theological foundation in our first part and, in the second part, to devote it to practice.

A Trinitarian theological foundation is necessary, I believe, because if at the bottom of who we are, or at the core of who we are is our life in God, there has to be something further below ourselves, holding it all together as its life and flow. And that is God Trinity's own life, which is a sharing love, as expressed in 1 John 4:8, "God is love." The Greek is *"ho theos agape estin,"* or God is *agape*, "sharing love."

Could not the sharing love of 1 John apply to both the shared inner love and life of God Trinity as well as application to ourselves, who receive life as love for participation? Humanity is the image of God (Genesis 1:26), and as the image of God, humans are relational because God is relational. Our life with God Trinity is one of invitation and response, mirroring the inner sharing life of God. As God's children we are made for that communion now with our brothers and sisters and God, consummating in the communion of eternity, a seamless love, to which we respond in our moment.

The love relationship might be imagined as persons facing one other. When we love honestly in a range of possible human relationships, simply being in the other's presence can evoke a loving presence in return. And so prayer is like that as well, a simple attentive presence, a gaze into our heart or center of who we are. We can't study or think our way there. Reflective reading and meditative thought are so helpful in preparing and disposing us for the Spirit's activity within us. The Holy Spirit is given us to bring us to our true selves and to a loving communion within, inviting in us a response.

A tapestry provides an image of God's invitation woven in with the response of humanity. And a deeper weave is also present, of the very life of God Trinity. Our weaving with God is sustained by the master weave of the inner life of God.

Eastern Christian theology presents a cooperative synergy, *synergeia*, between God and the human person. Given the complexities and contradictions in life, it may often appear as if we are on the back side of the tapestry, noting threads hanging and directionless. We are given moments when we can see the pattern from the front side, here and there, its poetry and confidence. Christian prayer and life, living in the very *agape* love of God, is the weave of our life.

Over the last century, theology has had an important reconnection to Scripture and to the earliest Christian writers, for the sake of a continuum of theological conversation. That movement of recovery is called *ressourcement*, or return to these sources.

Theologian Yves Congar was a great advocate for the *ressourcement* approach and was himself steeped in the centuries of Christian theological discourse. Congar went beyond the written sources, attributing to Charles Péguy, who coined the term *ressourcement*, the conviction that we must return to the source of the written sources, which is God Trinity. We will return to Congar later for application of his study of the Holy Spirit's action.

Entering into the very life of God is the dignity of the human person and the glory of God. Expressed as a teaching, it is called divinization, or *theosis* in Greek, which arises in communion with God. St. Irenaeus of Lyons, the first systematic theologian, wrote that "the glory of God is the person fully alive, and the life of the person is communion with God."

Our tradition suggests that God Trinity can be likened to a great outward movement of love and a great inward movement of love. St. Thomas Aquinas is identified with an *exitus-reditus* or outward-inward structure to his theology. Perhaps inspired by Neo-Platonism, *exitus-reditus* has a captivating dynamic and poetic quality: the Word of God came forth in love to humanity to carry humanity into intimacy with God and to be the loving culmination of cosmic history. Today, other descriptive terms, such as God's outgoing centrifugal love and embracing and recapitulating centripetal love and a personalist invitation and response, are also available. Dynamic terms are essential; otherwise God becomes separate and static. This is a profound challenge and risk.

A twofold invitation and response is the pattern of our meditation method. I believe it is the pattern of the very life of God Trinity and the pattern of everything. When we are in accord with God's invitation and are beginning to respond, the promise of new and flourishing living emerges. Western theologians called right relationship "rectitude," and Eastern theologians saw the possibility of the person living rightly to live in a new paradisical state of purified heart and intention. The prayer of the heart and a quiet repose in the active love of God is prompted by the Holy Spirit for our progress in the way of response. Human flourishing is the fruit of the Spirit given to us. The Spirit is the first and greatest gift.

Integrating Spirituality in Contemplative Living

While we strive for integration in life, balance might be a struggle and can tend to overly compartmentalize: prayer is one area of awareness; relationships with others another area, as well as our approach to a just, ethical, or moral life. Soon the concerns can become isolated from one another and become their own boxes. After all, we can read a book devoted to prayer, relationships, justice, or the history of theology. In an integrative spirituality, prayer rests in God and manifests a Christian relationship to our sisters and brothers.

Within two millennia of Christian examples, Dorothy Day is near, and came to mind for her own integrated spirituality. She was a teacher of the Catholic justice tradition in action and a teacher of the contemplative life in the midst of lower Manhattan street sounds.

> I shall meditate as I have been accustomed, in the little Italian Church on Twelfth Street, by the side of the open window, looking out at the plants growing on the roof, the sweet corn, the boxes of herbs, the geraniums in bright bloom, and I shall rest happy in the presence of Christ on the altar, and then I shall come home and I shall write, as Pere Gratry advises, and try to catch some of the things that happen to bring me nearer to God, to catch them and put them down on paper.
>
> And because I am a woman involved in practical cares, I cannot give the first half of my day to these things, but must meditate when I can, early in the morning and on the fly during the day. Not in the privacy of a study – but here, there and everywhere – at the kitchen table, on the train, on the ferry, on my way to and from appointments and even while making supper and putting Teresa to bed.[13]

New York City churches in the early twentieth century had stained-glass windows that actually opened out below the image; it was before the era of enclosed buildings. When the days were pleasant enough, natural air and street sounds came in, especially when the heavy doors opened to the coming and goings of others for their visits; sacred space wasn't so walled off. Dorothy Day wrote of her happy and loving rest, present to Christ in the eucharist. And there she sat until she rose.

When I first read her reflection, I lived in my hometown of Paterson, New Jersey, about 15 miles from her Manhattan neighborhood. Paterson was one of the first industrial centers in the nation and home to vibrant immigrant groups and neighborhoods, similar to where Day lived. My parish church had that feel, and I imagined it was similar to where Dorothy Day sat—it could be dark by current standards—with the less bright lighting of the time and windows open to our street sounds, and so I felt connected to her shared neighborhood and experience and received her teaching. Located in a place with an inward and outward sense helped my foundational lived spirituality.

Dorothy Day represented both the interactive justice and spiritual traditions. She reflected the saints over the centuries; that love could not be walled off, a part for God and a part for neighbor, later. She came to find herself emerging over time with her own spiritual journey and personal integration.

Looking back, hers was the first compelling example of a "contemplative life." She helped me to see contemplative living all around me, in the many and varied Catholic persons in everyday living in our largely first-generation immigrant urban parish community of industrial Paterson.

God was somehow woven into our lives. Yet there were also voices that presented us as removed from God, and prayer could become distant praise and petition. Many of us might have been raised in a distant model; it became our default. But if humanity is planned by God for the intimacy of Trinitarian love, prayer can essentially be intimate. In all relationships, including prayer, intimacy requires intentionality and time.

Types of Christian Prayer

Prayer is a primary manifestation of faith relationship. Words are a natural expression in prayer but prayer should not be reduced to saying prayers. Prayer foundationally is within the relationship of faith, hope, and love, and so it is a rest within the rest of faith, with the Holy Spirit's active engagement in promoting and leading us, even in this moment, to receptivity and response. And so the character of rest in prayer is something of what Blessed John Ruusbroec would term an "active rest" within the active dynamic of Trinitarian love.

Blessed John returns again and again to prayer as rest. Rest is within the active love of the Trinity, and so relationality is implied. Prayer is aware relationality. Our model proposes a way of prayer that uses thoughts for our relational context in God Trinity but does not ultimately rely on words, ideas, or images. Within the great breadth of Christian spirituality, this is a path that is ancient but not often traveled. It invites our attention.

"Meditation" and "contemplation" flow naturally in the life of loving awareness as we follow God Trinity's lead inward. Thomas Merton provided a good working distinction between meditation and contemplation—that is, the simple distinction that "meditation" is what we do and "contemplation" is what God gives. Merton wrote about the Western practice of "discursive meditation" or "mental prayer" that begins with recollection and rational reflection, or reading a topic to open ourselves to the working of the Holy Spirit. He opened the way of meditation to the faithful in the mid-twentieth century; his influence is lasting. It was my foundational practice of meditation for decades.

For the majority of Christians, "meditation" and "contemplation" can seem off-putting, reserved to monastics. Dorothy Day demonstrated otherwise as she wrote that her life and work didn't permit "the first half of the day … in the privacy of a study" but woven in, "on the fly" in her life—a contemplative life.

Meditation and contemplation, because the Spirit both leads us to and responds to our response, were woven into Dorothy Day's self-understanding. Thus, if "meditation" and "contemplation" need a recovery in our lives, Dorothy Day can help. She was an outstanding example of the active life, yet saw it coming from a deeper inner integration, a growing relationship with God.

Meditation has many different shapes, as there have been manifold "schools" of spirituality, often identified with religious orders in the Christian East and West. They developed within the cultural influences of their time and blended with intersectionality. Ours, too, is a way of meditation arising from human intersectionality and prompted, I believe, by the Holy Spirit.

In a renewed and accessible manner, "mysticism" might be seen as a deep form of contemplation that brings a profound vision of everyday life, a unique insight and integration, accompanied by peace. It is a gift and action of the Holy Spirit, and our experiences of the wisdom given by the Spirit should prompt a simple "Glory be to you, O Lord" arising from our hearts. Mysticism should not be an off-putting term. A mystic vision is integrated loving insight to the moment and then to the whole as unity, freely given by the Spirit.

Irish Jesuit William Johnston, ministering in Japan, encountered intersectionality. Johnston, like Karl Rahner and other twentieth-century theologians, was alarmed that God was increasingly becoming an object of intellectual assent, and prayer something of an add-on. God was becoming extrinsic to the human person, and so, too, was prayer.

Rahner returned to Scripture's recognition of God's breath in creation as "the divine life-giving force" that is understood over time to be the gift of eternal life. Rahner presents God's self-bestowal and "self-communication to the rational creature by the grace of God's *pneuma* as the highest, freely given unsurpassable step and phase of this one evolution."[14]

The turn to theological self-understanding certainly entails the intellectual but lives by an inner shift to the spirit and heart, taking us inward, each of us, to encounter in the life-giving God Trinity of every moment, "on the fly," "on the train," and "making supper" with Dorothy Day. We are not alone; rather, we are accompanied and indwelt.

St. Paul's Elevator Speech

If one has a small window of opportunity to present a potential plan or significant thought to someone, one would estimate the limited time and the essential points to make. The statement should be clear and quite bold. It is known as an "elevator speech" or "elevator pitch," imagining the transit of a minute or so on an elevator between the floors of an office building.

St. Paul's brief speech at the Areopagus in Athens has those qualities of the well-planned words for maximum effect in a brief amount of time. He appreciated the altar "to an unknown god" and wanted to share his good news and message:

> Athenians, I see how extremely religious you are in every way.... The God who made the world and everything in it, he who is Lord of heaven and earth, does not live in shrines made by human hands, nor is he served by human hands, as though he needed anything,

since he himself gives to all mortals life and breath and all things.... He is not far from each one of us. For "In him we live and move and have our being"; as even some of your own poets have said, "For we too are his offspring."[15]

Paul introduced his faith relationship in a God who is not distant and extrinsic; "in him we live and move and have our being." Paul uses "life and breath" as given by God, who personally and lovingly animates. His message could be heard afresh by contemporary Christians; we take it to heart here.

Cosmogenesis, Incompleteness of the World, and Its Consummation

Integration of the faith and mystical vision with astrophysics can support the contemplative life and imagination. Denis Edwards, an Australian theologian, is quite taken by the opportunity to weave God's action and God's breath in contemporary science. He traces the evolution of the cosmos and the explosions of stars to form our carbon-based world and carbon-based humanity. He finds humanity to be "animated dust," which gives an interesting new appreciation of the dust God animates by breathing into it in Genesis.[16] Dynamically oriented to God, perhaps we are "divinized dust."

Animated as we are, we are mortal. Death is an enigma; we are enlivened by God's very Breath, but as mortal, "a mere breath" (Psalm 37). For Rahner, Christianity is not a religion that denies mortality but is oriented to the consummation in eternity. St. Paul, in his letter to the Romans, framed our Christian understanding of feeling the touch of divinity and the touch of mortality. Paul does it with an eye to the yearning of creation, as well as the indwelling Spirit's fostering prayer in the moment:

> For the creation waits with eager longing for the revealing of the children of God.... We know that the whole creation has been groaning in labor pains until now; and not only the creation, but we ourselves who have the first fruits of the Spirit, groan inwardly

while we wait for adoption, the redemption of our bodies.... Likewise, the Spirit helps us in our weakness; for we do not know how to pray as we ought, but that very Spirit intercedes with sighs too deep for words. (Romans 8:19, 22–23, 26)

Paul's attentiveness to the activity of the Spirit was characteristic of early Christians, and we can read his words as an invitation to renewed relationship. It makes all the difference.

Notes

1. John Ruusbroec, "The Little Book of Clarification," in *John Ruusbroec: The Spiritual Espousals and Other Works*, introduction and translation by James A. Wiseman, OSB (New York: Paulist Press, 1985), 263. He is "Blessed John," a recognition of the reliability of his teaching and personal spiritual life in 1908. His liturgical feast day is December 2, based on his death on December 2, 1381.

2. William Johnston, *The Still Point: Reflections on Zen and Christian Mysticism* (New York: Harper and Row, 1971). Johnston presented Zen for significant spiritual theological engagement with the West. The Catholic monastics Aelred Graham and Bede Griffiths also lived in the East and had important introductory roles for the West.

3. William Johnston, "Christian Zen," in *Lord Teach Us to Pray* (London: Fount, 1991), 88.

4. Martin Laird, *Into the Silent Land: A Guide to the Christian Practice of Contemplation* (New York: Oxford University Press, 2006). James Finley, *Christian Meditation: Experiencing the Presence of God; A Guide to Contemplation* (New York: Harper One, 2004).

5. Ruben L.F. Habito, *The Healing Breath of Zen* (Boston: Wisdom Publications, 2006), 55.

6. Paul F. Knitter, *Without Buddha I Could Not Be a Christian* (London: Oneworld Publications, 2015), 156–57.

7. Louis Hughes, OP, *The Art of Allowing: The Breath in Meditation and in Life* (Blackrock, Co. Dublin: The Columba Press, 2010). Fr. Hughes engages our body in breathing, in his Christian application from yoga practice, and his appendices give a very effective, concise analysis of Cartesian philosophy and the significance of breath in ancient languages. Johnston, Habito, Knitter, and Hughes are all keenly aware of the presence of the Holy Spirit within the breath for Christians. Johnston turns in a robust manner to theological voices such as St. Thomas Aquinas and Karl Rahner, based on his work in the history of Christian spirituality.

8   John Ruusbroec lived at a time of crises on social, political, and ecclesial levels, but with important elements of spiritual practice. Ruusbroec was a priest who retreated with colleagues to a monastic community near Brussels. He was engaged in conversation with the vibrant Flemish communities and is thought to have known the Dominican John Tauler. Louis Dupré calls Ruusbroec "the most articulate Trinitarian mystic of the Western Church" (Wiseman, *John Ruusbroec*, xi). Ruusbroec is a prime guide for our reflection.

9   Tomas Spidlik, *Spirituality of the Christian East*, trans. Anthony P. Gythiel (Kalamazoo, MI: Cistercian Publications, 1986), 20. This study is a valuable guide. Spidlik was a Cardinal in the Catholic Church. He notes that when the Messalian movement overemphasized experience of God and needed correction, the ancient Eastern church never denied the ongoing active presence of the Holy Spirit.

10 Mindfulness practice was initiated by Jon Kabat-Zinn, PhD, as Mindfulness-Based Stress Reduction (MBSR) for medical patients, which is having a tremendous benefit for persons. MBSR is based on breath practice. More recently, practices that combine breath with compassion development include Cognitive Based Compassion Training (CBCT), a secular practice inspired by the teaching of the Dalai Lama; this author completed the course.

11 St. Elizabeth of the Trinity, Carmelite, *I Have Found God. Complete Works, Volume II: Letters from Carmel*, trans. Anne Englund Nash (Washington, DC: ICS Publications, Institute for Carmelite Studies, 1995), 358.

12 Karl Rahner, "The Spirituality of the Church of the Future," in *Concern for the Church: Theological Investigations XX*, trans. Edward Quinn (New York: Crossroad, 1981), 149. Rahner based his theological studies on Christian anthropology, which was in turn based on Trinitarian theology, with a mystical understanding of Trinitarian unity.

13 Dorothy Day, *Meditations*, selected and arranged by Stanley Vishnewski (New York: Paulist Press, 1970), 6.

14 Karl Rahner, "The Secret of Life," in *Theological Investigations VI*, trans. Karl-H. and Boniface Kruger (Baltimore: Helicon; and London: Darton, Longman & Todd, 1969), 144–49. Rahner uses Scriptural language for God's Breath/Spirit, freely: *ruach/ruah, pneuma*, spirit.

15 Acts 18:22, 24–25, 27b–28. All Scripture is *New Revised Standard Version* (NRSV) unless otherwise noted.

16 Denis Edwards, *Breath of Life: A Theology of the Holy Spirit* (Maryknoll, NY: Orbis Books, 2004). Referenced here for his attention to contemporary science, Edwards provides an important study of the Holy Spirit.

PART I

Foundations for Practice

INVITATION-RESPONSE IN SHARED LOVE might be called an inner dynamic, as far as the modest limits of words and thoughts can take us, of the inner life of God Trinity. Our theological reflection is for the sake of our own self-understanding and for our entry into the invitation-response dynamic of the Trinity.

Part I consists of foundations and includes three major parts: *Breathe*, *Receive*, and *Respond*. Part I is set in motion in Part II ("Practice"), with its elements of *Breathing*, *Receiving*, and *Responding*. There is just a bit of repetition to facilitate the introduction for the sake of application in practice. Part III, "Living with Ourselves and Others," is a conclusion that is oriented to practice.

Our goal is to provide an introduction to a model that is fulfilled in prayer practice.

CHAPTER 1

Breathe

CHRISTIANITY IS REALLY AN incarnational experience, and in earliest centuries was vibrantly experienced as such. It is worth recovering. The water of baptism is the encounter with living water for new life in Christ, the oil of confirmation and chrismation is our being sealed, protected, and preserved by the Holy Spirit, and in Eucharist God self-gives for a profound moment of communion, abiding now and pledging the future banquet of the New Jerusalem.

The list could proceed through the sacraments to the sacramental encounters of everydayness, to icons and statues we live with and which remind us of ourselves, to Scripture that we hold and hear, in kisses with spouses and family, the warmth of friendship, an openness to all persons as sisters and brothers, to gratitude for the cosmos and earth, animal companions, the food before us, and loving receptivity of gratitude in every moment.

We live in discrete moments of time yet can develop a sense of time's flow and ourselves within it in the stages of life. Integrating activity has an intellectual dimension, of course, and is completed by a certain interior sense we have and which can become more animated. Interiority doesn't take us into a parallel universe to the spheres of intellect or action, but integrates us to everything.

We know our interior self is there because we've experienced it at times, when we've sensed things coming together in a deep unity that overcomes usual barriers and definitions; such can be a moment of experiencing transcendence. Transcendence can be the experience of boundarylessness given by the Spirit. Transcendence can effect radical inclusion and is most profound when the inclusion is the dynamism of love that is God's vision or reign.

Inclusiveness of transcendence happens in our interiority: where we most deeply live and where God lives within us. Interiority is often called inner life, the heart, spirit, or soul. The Latin word for soul is *anima*, which gets directly into English as animation; *anima* is life, our inner life. We tend to think of soul as being something ghostly and thus have trouble making sense of it. But our medieval ancestors said *anima animat*; the soul/*anima* animates. It is not a place of distraction or hiding out, but how God animates us and nudges us toward the good and loving and inclusive, which is God's way or reign.

This is where the breath comes in. Breath was identified with God's animation of the soil-based carbon (*adamah*) called Adam in the creation account of Genesis. God's own breath is given to Adam and is a primary sign to humanity of God's intimacy.

Hebrew *ruah* is breath or wind blowing without restraint. Biblical scholar Richard Clifford, SJ, defines *ruah* as "air in motion," hence "wind," "breath," "spirit."[1] Genesis was developed over centuries and is not the earliest book of the Bible, though it is presented first. Breath was already a settled and familiar image for divine action. God's *ruah*, which could be dramatic or intimate, might have been a more effective approach to God than another idea about God.

John McKenzie found that in the theology of the Old Testament, the breath or spirit is communicated to human beings, yet remains God's own:

> The breath of Yahweh is the principle of life for all living beings; they survive by the communication of his spirit. This thought appears in a number of passages (Gen 2:7; 6:17; 7:15; Job 33:4; Eccl 3:19, 21). The breath of life is communicated by inspiration (Gen 2:7), and the living being dies when Yahweh takes away his spirit (Ps 104:29), which then returns to Yahweh (Eccl 12:7).[2]

Robert Alter translated the Psalms and comments on Psalm 94, verse 30: "When You send forth Your breath, they are created, and You renew the face of the earth." He notes the word *nefesh* or "breath" in this verse: "The Hebrew term equally means 'spirit,' but the background of Genesis argues for the sense of 'breath' because it is God's breath there that brings life into being."[3]

The creation account of Genesis was a response to Mesopotamian narratives positing humanity as a result of conflict among warring cosmic forces. Judaism's account was quite the opposite of cosmic clash. The point of Genesis was God's intentional, intimate, and loving relationship with all creation and humanity in particular, called to loving relationship and animated by God's own breath.

Richard Clifford's scholarly commentary on Genesis has a poetic quality; he found that the statement of creation is also a statement of the end, God's intent for harmony and peace:

> Gen 1 [Genesis chapter 1] stays within the categories of the "science" of its time and attempts to see in those categories divine power and purpose, and the unique place of humans. Conflict between chaotic forces (sea, darkness) which characterizes many other biblical and Near Eastern accounts, is absent. There seems even to be a polemic against such conflict cosmogonies. Creation follows effortlessly from God's mere word. Because Gen 1 is a portrait of what God intends, it is also an eschatological statement. This serene, beautiful world, in which all is ordered to humans, and humans are ordered to God, is how it will be at the end. The stories of human sin, which follow Gen 1, cannot permanently disfigure the original divine intent; God's world will triumph. Rev 21–22, the description of God's new world, appropriately draws on this chapter.[4]

God creates for relationship and communion with creatures called God's image in Genesis 1:26. As salvation history unfolds, God guides the path of Israel to Mary, who in representing the *anawim*, or the poor and utterly disposed, to Yahweh, accepts her pivotal role as Mother of the Incarnate Word. Jesus, the Word, and the Breath-Spirit of God are revealed as the inviters, gifts, and sustainers of life in God Trinity.

The earliest Christians expected an imminent return of Jesus in glory. Over time, the understanding grew that divine participation given in the Word and the Breath is not deferred to the end of history but is present now in "realized eschatology." We are in this fullness now; it is within us as the source of life. The great hymns at the start of the Letters to the Colossians and Ephesians sing the cosmic role of the Word as the way to the goal of God's peace that Genesis begins to reveal. We can choose to work on integrating the cosmic vision of our early Christian ancestors.

Richard Clifford appreciated the ancient world's comfort with multiple accounts of the same event—for example, Genesis has a creation narrative in chapter one and another in chapter two, the stories of two editorial traditions. In chapter one, beasts, birds, and creeping things have the breath in life. In the first account, a creature bearing the very image of God appears. The second chapter carries the animation of breath to Adam: "... then the LORD God formed man from the dust of the ground, and breathed into his nostrils the breath of life; and the man became a living being" (Gen 2:7).

Breath has a significant and powerful function as a symbol of relationship from the start of creation. A key and core suggestion of this study is to enter into breath as symbol of our identity in God Trinity.

Symbol is at risk of being devalued as something separate and less than reality, in other words, "only a symbol." However, symbol has a wealth of levels of meaning: the immediate as well as a way to a fullness.

Karl Rahner saw a symbol as having meaning in itself and pointing beyond itself to even deeper meaning. Imagine the key to a door as symbol. It has meaning in and of itself, but the key points beyond itself to a lock, and if this key and this lock are in fact paired, a new space opens.

Ruah and *nefesh* in Genesis have that quality as symbol, I believe. It opens us up to existential awareness of God's intimacy in the breath I take and receive now.

Appreciation of breath as God's intimacy and proximity to humanity was well established, and the Hebrew words for life-breath carry this sense.

With a next step in the future of our tradition, I believe that breath has a message for us and a deep symbolic opening. It may be helpful for contemporary Christians to encounter breathing practice in Trinitarian spirituality and prayer. Thus, our renewed understanding of breath must be intentional, suspending our own reductionist sense of the process of respiration as a biological function.

We are not alone in this recovery. Some of the earliest Christian theologians made frequent reference to God's presence in our breath. The Jewish Scriptures were keenly aware of our humanity, yet repeatedly saw God's intimacy in the breath.

Our medieval Christian ancestors returned to the image and symbol of breath for relationship with God. There are countless examples. For instance, St. Hildegarde of Bingen describes herself as a feather on the breath of God.

What can we take away from this? Breath is the symbol of God's intimacy and presence in the human person. And that breath, which has meaning in itself, can, as a symbol, open us to an even greater experience, and in contemplative practice, open us and dispose us to the action of the Spirit in us.

Biblical Hebrew *ruah* and Greek *pneuma* can be used interchangeably to reference wind (we should include cosmic wind), and breath, and spirit, and God's Spirit. *Ruah* and *pneuma*, or breath and spirit, have often been translated as spirit, which has both a justification as well as a risk of isolating the creative power of God's breath to an abstraction. Abstractions can sap its power and inhibit God's Spirit.

By coming closer to the biblical meaning and power of the words, I believe we should recognize "spirit" as being polyvalent, having separate, distinguishable powers or capacities.

Valence is a term from the scientific lexicon that references strengths and capacities. "Spirit" requires recognition of its cosmic power and intimacy to us ... and that it also carries the intimacy and actual, existential indwelling in us of the Holy Spirit, the Holy Breath of God. Henceforth, when we read translations of *pneuma* or *ruah* in Scripture, we might be aware of the valence, the force, of the word.

In the New Testament letters, sacred authors used the word *pneuma* as a default translation of "spirit" but isn't necessarily so. A meditative pause to recognize Spirit-given and Breath-given as God's Self-given can only open us more to its manifold valences. Open to understanding, yes, and more to encounter, reception, and response.

A final consideration of this chapter looks forward to the next, as well as begins the practical application of breathing. I place breathe within receive, as breath is received, and I pair receive with respond, as the pattern of Christian life practice, inclusive of self, God Trinity, and our brothers and sisters.

Even now, might I suggest a practice of aware and intentional breathing? It is critical to move breath from abstraction to practice. Openness to the Spirit will follow in a developmental manner. First is intentional and received breath, blossoming as received breath becomes prayer in a foundational way and breath-Spirit reception becomes critical for Christian living in enlightenment and in love.

Openness to this practice will lead to ongoing brief reconnection through the course of the day by self-remembering. It will bring us to our moment, as Dorothy Day wrote, for contemplation on the fly. Be aware and patient, as your initial practice of breathing might take some time and dedication. Ancient Christians would go to the desert for spiritual restoration and thereby learned dependence on God's animating presence. Time dedicated to learning breathing practice might be seen as the equivalent of going to the desert, even though you might simply be in your room, and come to be there in a new way.

Breathing practice in your experience of Christian life may be intended by God to be something enjoyed as natural and progress to a loving receptivity and response. Breathing meditation is practice for integrated human appreciation and spirituality; it doesn't have to remain a physical practice alone.

A widely used method: In a quiet place, sitting gently upright is recommended. We start slowly, with a minute or two of intentional focused breathing; as you breathe, allow your shoulders to slightly and naturally relax. You may find the need to progress to ten- and twenty-minute periods of simple attention (and recovered attention) to the breath and its serenity.

It is quite important to develop a facility for the practice; we will vary by personality and experience in the ability to live with our breath. Once progressed, our breath awareness will come back to us within seconds. We want to breathe with awareness and attention to the breath by entering into it, and not so much thinking about the breath. It's good to think about breath while you're reading this, of course, but gentle received breathing lets us enter into breath.

We are relearning breathing. Give it time and use it when there aren't a million different things on your mind. Over time, we can use every opportunity that presents itself, such as lying in bed for a few moments of quiet breathing, lying straight, before rising, to return to God in ourselves. Checking electronic messages in bed can wait a few minutes; breathing prayer and spiritual orientation to the day comes first.

As time goes on we will apply our breathing practice in walking, eating, washing up, and in everyday relationships. Breath will come to be a way of self-remembering and self-presenting to others, even in difficult moments and conversations as part of our response, in this moment.

Notes

1. Richard Clifford, SJ, "Genesis," in *New Jerome Biblical Commentary*, ed. Raymond Brown, SS; Joseph Fitzmyer, SJ; Roland Murphy, OCarm (Englewood Cliffs, NJ: Prentice Hall, 1990), 10.

2. John L. McKenzie, "Aspects of Old Testament Thought," in *New Jerome Biblical Commentary*, ed. Raymond Brown, SS; Joseph Fitzmyer, SJ; Roland Murphy, OCarm (Englewood Cliffs, NJ: Prentice Hall, 1990), 1290.

3. Robert Alter, *The Book of Psalms: A Translation with Commentary* (New York and London: W.W. Norton and Company, 2007), 367, n.29. He also writes of the difficult work of translation, that *nefesh* is "life breath," which became *anima* in the Vulgate and "soul" in the King James; "Introduction," xxxii.

4. Clifford, "Genesis," 11.

CHAPTER 2

Receive

Breathe is immediately related to, within, and for the sake of Receive, and then to Respond. In the previous chapter, "Breathe," breath is proposed as having a deep symbolic quality. Rahner's understanding of symbol is helpful. Symbol has both meaning in itself as well as carrying us to more. Receive-Respond is the dynamic within the Trinity as well as our life in and with God. Breathe is given particular attention as being within the Receive dynamic.

Here, *Breathe* facilitates *Receive*. In the breathing practice of the world's religious and wisdom traditions, persons have the gift of initiating breath, as well as the quality of intentionally or mindfully receiving breath. And in prayer formed with a biblical understanding, by receiving the breath mindfully we can become recollected and dispose ourselves to receive God, the intimate giver of breath in prayer and in life.

Breathe-Receive reminds me of the spirit of the nineteenth-century Carmelite nun St. Thérèse of Lisieux, who proposed the "little way" of spirituality. She did not see herself ascending to God as much as being carried into God. Our loving reception of breath as God's intimate animation can be a simple and small way of love that, over time, will move beyond thought to loving gratitude in the heart.

Significance of Reception in Christian Teaching and Life

Perhaps this is a surprising statement, but we are in a position to explore our reception of breath in a spiritual manner or with meditative awareness as a way to receive God. Reception is not a stray skill among others; rather, it lies at the core of Christian anthropology. Nor are we imposing sacred teaching on breath practice. Rather, within our tradition, we are finding the deepest and most significant sacred reality within the breath.

Our invitation to Christian breath response arises from the dynamic of the inner life of God Trinity, the real beneath, beyond, and pervading the empirically real. And so our reception of breath is the entryway to our self-disposal for an experiential awareness of our life in Trinitarian communion.

Words about God Trinity Love's inner life can have a meaningful directionality, yet the first Christian theologians stated that their words by necessity always fall short of God. St. John of Damascus (+749) was an early theologian who was foundational to the Eastern and Western Churches. When he used words to share sacred teaching, he referenced the limitation of thought and words: "... not all things are inexpressible and not all are capable of expression...."[1]

Even his statements of limitations of thought and word have a poetic sense: "... God is without beginning and without end, everlasting and eternal, uncreated, unchangeable, inalterable, simple, uncompounded, incorporeal, invisible, impalpable, uncircumscribed, unlimited, incomprehensible, uncontained, unfathomable, good, just, the maker of all created things...."[2] For us, "uncircumscribed" might be the most challenging, because God cannot be finally pinned down and managed.

And so, all so gingerly, words take us to the giving and receiving in the life of God Trinity. What words might take us into the mystery of God? Karl Rahner was so taken with the simple expression of 1 John 4:8: "God is love." *Ho theos agape estin.*

Agape is the critical Greek word. *Agape* is a sharing love. The sharing is found in the God Trinity before time and extended to the cosmos and humanity with the creation of the space-time continuum.

But can we say that sharing and receiving are part of the inner life of God? Just one example is found in John 17:7, when Jesus declares: *Now they know that everything you have given me is from you.* Rather than a passing comment, this statement of Jesus about his loving relationship to the Father turns theological reflection to the Father as the Source of Love, begetting the Son in Love and for Love. At the end of the chapter, Jesus, filled with *agape* love, concludes the Last Supper discourse with: "I made your name known to them, and I will make it known, so that the love with which you have loved me may be in them, and I in them."

And so, our quality to receive is not something secondary but a divine quality that is in the very pattern of God Trinity. Reception begins in the very communion of the persons of the Trinity, before time, before creation, in the generation of the second person, the Word, Jesus by God in Fatherhood.

Reception (and generous giving love, *agape*) begins within the being of God Trinity. We are patterned to receive and give as a result. Given the empirical self-understanding of our time, our default might be to see ourselves as fairly autonomous entities in a biochemical descriptor, originating awareness, attitudes, and actions within ourselves. At first blush this might have accurate elements, but does it amount to a suitable account or even one with the right foundational elements?

From its earliest days, based on Scripture, Christian teaching presents our own receptivity as not distant from but utterly and fundamentally woven into our identity, God's intent in creating humanity for reception of individual being, yet not separated from being-in-communion with God on the way to eternal consummation of unity. The contemplative theological tradition has quietly kept this alive over the centuries.

Normative and historically defined Christian speech recognizes that God Trinity does not need time as a basis for action; the Latin root of "eternal" means "outside of time" or "away from time." When we speak of God the Father's begetting of the Son in love and the procession of the Spirit in love from the Father to the Son, we are not referring to temporal and extrinsic acts happening outside God, but eternally within and constituting Trinitarian life. We can reflect on the generosity of the Father and the receptivity of the Son. For us, entering into the receptivity of the Word spoken by God can foster our human capacity to consciously, and by enlightenment, enter into the life offered by God Trinity.

Jesus models and teaches orientation to his Father and helps us enter into this relationship by the simple and profound prayer with his invocation "Abba" in the "Our Father" prayer. Early Christians are said to have prayed it three times a day. Could it ground them in reception from Jesus for relationship with the Father and dedication to the cause of the Father?

Jesus is a bridge or circle, an *exitus* and *reditus*, outgoing and returning, in his coming from the Father and return with us to the Father.

A deeper appreciation of the eternal receptivity of the *Verbum*, or Word of God, the second person of the Trinity, begotten before time, carries us to awareness of the Holy Spirit. Dominican theologian Yves Congar was a principal theologian of the Second Vatican Council, a scholar of Thomas Aquinas, and historical theologian. Congar wrote of the Holy Spirit as Breath and always in relation to the Father and the Son: "He is the communion between the Father and the Son, but he is first of all the Breath of God. The Son is the Image, but he is first of all the Word coming from the mouth of the Father and accompanied by the Breath, and therefore accompanied by a power that sets things in motion."[3]

Christian doctrine uses expressions of the Father as source, provider, and goal; the Son as exemplar, and the Spirit as giver of life and love. Congar uses the lovely image of Christ as *Head* of his body; the gathered Church and the Spirit as *Heart* of the Church, animating them and the entire cosmos; the Spirit given for the future of the Church and the world.

Missions of the Word and the Breath

Father, Son, and Spirit–Breath are inseparably united from eternity. Our understanding of the missions of the Son and Spirit might benefit from renewal. We celebrate the mission of the Word at Christmas and the mission of the Breath at Pentecost, and as the Risen Jesus promises another advocate who will be given to bear fruit in us, the two missions are in unity.

St. Irenaeus of Lyons, one generation of teachers away from St. John the Evangelist, could be called the first systematic theologian. Irenaeus expressed the unified missions of Word and Breath in a simple image that seems unsurpassed. He called Jesus and the Holy Spirit "the two hands of God"—employed, as Congar puts it, "to fashion his creation."[4]

Irenaeus's expression captures our imagination and suggests both the presence of the Father with the "two hands" as truly Trinitarian, as well as our own embrace by the "two hands" in faith, hope, and love. The two hands represent both the work and missions, as well as the final goal of the missions: communion in God Trinity Love. This embrace is enlightening and can be the basis for a connection to Trinitarian life, our spirituality. Our prayer practice is inspired by the two hands, two missions, and the embrace in Trinitarian love. The embrace includes us as we are, for our ongoing response and actualization in love, and turning to our brothers and sisters.

Jesus, the Word Disclosed as the Beloved ... Ourselves Disclosed as the Beloved

Humanity was on God's mind for communion before time. The opening section of St. Paul's Letters to the Colossians and the Ephesians proclaim it.

Jennifer Berenson notes that the first section of chapter one of Ephesians "gives a sweeping overview of God's plan for salvation."[5] The letters reflect the late and most mature theology of Paul. Scholarly discussion continues whether the letters were written by Paul or his disciples while he was alive, or writing in his voice years after his death. The letters are part of the canon of Scripture and held to be inspired by the Spirit.

In addition, opening sections of the letters that will be cited were hymns of the early community; might such diminish their standing for some? Yet the Spirit may have led the composition of the hymns, then adopted by the author of the letters, increasing their significance by witnessing to the dynamic Christology alive in the community. Beyond that, the proclamation of the divine significance of humanity, found in hymns, makes them stand out to me even more. These early communities sang the meaning of humanity chosen in Christ from eternity!

From the hymn in Colossians 1:15–18: "He is the image of the invisible God, the firstborn of all creation; for in him all things in heaven and on earth were created, things visible and invisible, whether thrones or dominations or rulers or powers—all things have been created through him and for him. He himself is before all things, and in him all things hold together."

Throughout the writings of Paul, "in Christ" is stressed, and reflecting on its use, "in Christ" is more than an expression simply to be read, but instead a central and dynamic concept. Christ Jesus incarnate, risen and glorified, is the fullness of divinity with a "pan-cosmic" presence and power, as Rahner put it. A former student of the great German Scripture scholar Rudolf Schnackenburg told me that a prime exam question for graduate students was to ask the two driving words of St. Paul's Christology. The answers were elegantly simple: the words "in" and "through" Christ.

"In Christ" invites a foundational translation to personal spirituality. This is Paul's intention. A few lines later, after the Colossians hymn, a personalization of being "in Christ" is now expressed as Christ in us—not a reversal, but an interweaving. It makes very clear that God is not distant and extrinsic to humans, but a revelation that is "the mystery that has been hidden throughout the ages and generations but has now been revealed" to the Jewish people and now the Gentiles: "which is Christ in you, the hope of glory"(1:26–27).

In the Ephesians hymn, verses 3–10 of the first chapter stress being in Christ. Life and healing working through Christ appear again, and strongly. If this was a hymn of the early Church, it shares a cosmic vision of Christ before all and the fulfillment of all, or Christ the alpha and omega, and Christ the gatherer:

> Blessed be the God and Father of our Lord Jesus Christ, who has blessed us in Christ with every spiritual blessing in the heavenly places, just as he chose us in Christ before the foundation of the world to be holy and blameless before him in love. He destined us for adoption as his children through Jesus Christ, according to the good pleasure of his will, to the praise of his glorious grace that he

freely bestowed on us in the Beloved. In him we have redemption through his blood, the forgiveness of our trespasses, according to the riches of his grace that he lavished on us. With all wisdom and insight he has made known to us the mystery of his will, according to his good pleasure that he set forth in Christ, as a plan for the fullness of time, to gather up all things in him, things in heaven and things on earth.

A cosmic account of humanity emerges. It would inspire a contemporary theologian like Rahner to identify humanity as "God's project," rather than accepting an empirical account of our physical dimension with an extrinsic overlay of sin and redemption. Rahner was right to do so, and this is an encouragement for our own personal self-understanding, translating from a "Christian anthropology" to our lived experience. His global statement can be applied to ourselves as individuals and part of God's work. We have been chosen in the dynamism of Christ, who is template, form, and goal of human existence.

Rahner frequently stated that humanity was in God's mind and plan, even the generation of the Word from the Father. His theological speculation may be rooted in and is certainly supported by God's Word in the Ephesians hymn: "just as he chose us in Christ before the foundation of the world to be holy and blameless before him in love"(v. 4). That we are "before the foundation of the world," in Christ, can be a basis for our relational prayer life in God Trinity.

Standing out as profound for our lived awareness is Paul's identification of Jesus the Beloved with ourselves, humanity. In verse 5, we find the statement "He destined us for adoption as his children through Jesus Christ," which draws us intimately into Trinitarian life as children in and through Christ. Yet the following sentence (in v. 6) takes it to an even higher level: that this adoption is "to the praise of his glorious grace that he freely bestowed on us in the Beloved."

"In the Beloved" evokes attention and then awe. A spiritual reading attentive to the movement of the Spirit does not permit us to breeze through it. If Jesus is the only-begotten Son, and we too are recognized as children in Christ, and as Jesus is the Beloved, then through grace/gift/self-bestowal of God we are Beloved in the

Beloved. Beloved is our identity. Beloved is our foundation for personal development and relationality. Thanks be to God.

In my own reflection and life's trials, self-recognition and living as Beloved in the Beloved uniquely arose from the writings of Henri Nouwen. He transformed Belovedness from abstraction to life relationship for me, first through *Life of the Beloved*, and then *The Return of the Prodigal Son* and in an interview with Philip Roderick, in *Beloved: Henri Nouwen in Conversation*.[6]

Life of the Beloved is precious to many persons who have endured trials and found a new identity and relationship with God that is deep beneath thoughts and experiences, even of God and self. An irony of the book is that Nouwen was writing it for a friend he met through his work, a Jewish man not practicing his faith, yet admiring the way faith nurtured Henri.

As it was intended for all persons, including those without a religious tradition that actively nourishes them, *Life of the Beloved* was written with a minimal number of religious references. Nouwen tells Fred Bratman, for whom the book is written, that as he prepared to write something for him and his friends,

> I have been wondering if there might be one word I would most want you to remember when you finished reading all I wish to say. Over the past year, that special word has gradually emerged from the depths of my own heart. It is the word "Beloved," and I am convinced that it has been given to me for the sake of you and your friends. Being a Christian, I first learned this word from the story of the baptism of Jesus of Nazareth. "No sooner had Jesus come out of the water than he saw the heavens torn apart and the Spirit, like a dove, descending on him. And a voice came from heaven: 'You are my Son, the Beloved, my favor rests on you'" (Matt. 3:16–17; Mark 1:10–11; Luke 3:21–22). For many years I had read these words and even reflected on them in sermons and lectures, but it is only since our talks in New York that they have taken on a meaning far beyond the boundaries of my own tradition. Our many conversations led me to the inner conviction that the words "You are my Beloved" revealed the most intimate truth about all human beings, whether they belong to any particular tradition or not.[7]

The book found its greatest readership among persons of Christian faith who needed and longed for a foundational relationship of life with God. Nouwen then expresses that his "only desire is to make these words reverberate in every corner of your being—'You are the Beloved.'"[8]

In later interviews, Nouwen urged that our identity as the Beloved not be an abstraction or a piece of data, but so essential that "we live from it." We live in a journey to accept ourselves as the Beloved. Nouwen believed that our greatest risk to well-being is self-rejection. Don't we have so many occasions when this temptation arises?

Allowing ourselves to be the Beloved is an inner quality that we are invited to receive from the Holy Spirit. Being Beloved might be a challenge, but it is ultimately liberating. Receiving ourselves as God's Beloved opens us all the more to the Holy Spirit's dynamic love; this reception of ourselves is wrapped up with receiving the Spirit. Reception is at the core of our spiritual life.

I believe that Nouwen had his self-doubts and learned the hard way that he is the Beloved, in his life of faith, which gives him such credibility. Nouwen shares as a brother. Living from and as the Beloved is work to which we will return in our practice section. For now, we can begin to journey with our identity as Beloved more intentionally. We can receive it over and over as we receive the breath.

"Beloved" has three scriptural bases for critical applications in our theory and practice. The first, of course, is the Baptism of Jesus, in the Synoptic Gospels cited by Nouwen. The second instance is application to ourselves, as found in the first chapter of Ephesians, that we are, in my words, Beloved in the Beloved. The third is the way we as Beloved are called to actualize our lives with each other; Colossians 3:12–18 stands out simply because Paul makes the appeal to us as Beloved!

In the end, these Scriptures carry three foundational meanings for our intellect and lived awareness: Jesus is the unique Beloved in eternity; before the foundation of the world we are chosen as Beloved in the Beloved; and thus we are named and summoned to live from it in the freedom of the daughters and sons of God.

My only reason for presenting these concepts is their actualization. My proposal is that awareness of being the Beloved will start as a thought and then become a realization and cause of joy in our spirit. Christian prayer and meditation call for ongoing growth in enlightened wisdom and knowledge through study for knowledge as awareness in prayer experience.

The Mission of the Holy Spirit: Breath of God and Giver of Life and Love

Actualization in life and love both in us and throughout the cosmos is the work of the Spirit. As the Breath of God and the mutual love of Father and Son, the Spirit processes in Trinitarian love and is bestowed in creation, sustaining and guiding to the consummation of creation in Trinitarian communion.

The Creed, hammered out in Christian antiquity, is proclaimed in Sunday gatherings of God's people over the centuries; "the Holy Spirit, Lord and Giver of Life" is significant. Can the new cosmology find a starting point of cosmic energy that is the work of Spirit, Lord and Giver of Life?

Our theological reflection on the Holy Spirit as Breath, Love, Gift, Giver of Life, and Actualizer supports awareness in our response in the Spirit for our life in God Trinity. Awareness is enlightenment for actualization in prayer relationship and its continuation in authentic, everyday life.

Our cultural context and received spirituality are that of the "modern world," a period that began several centuries ago and is now ending; it tended, under the influence of empiricism, to put God "out there." The modern out-there-ing of God shaped the thinking even of religious believers. Empiricism was a great advance for the development of the sciences and advances in the standard of living, including health improvement for countless persons. But empiricism tended to overreach in public discussion, claiming that the measurable is the standard of truth.

Recovering from an out-there God requires a stance toward God as source of cosmic energy as well as interior life. Classical Christian spirituality of the contemplative current is the inner life; hence reliance on the inner experience as it develops. Scholarship over the last century has renewed the ability to encounter early Christian understanding of Scripture, theology, and contemplative living.

For St. Paul, the missions of Christ the Word and the Holy Spirit, the Breath, can't be separated. They are, using Irenaeus's term, the two hands of God. Paul recognizes that the ongoing work of Jesus in the persons gathered as church and ourselves within the community is entrusted to the Holy Spirit. He writes that those who had come to believe in the gospel "were marked by the seal of the promised Holy Spirit" (Eph. 1:13). A seal protects, as the Spirit enwraps us unto the consummation of our life in God.

Confirmation or chrismation is identified as a sacramental instance of the seal of the Spirit. In practice, a seal has an ongoing protection that opens to the symbol of breath as the ongoing, intimate presence of the Spirit. Awareness of receiving the breath can be Spirit awareness and intimacy. It can grow as practice develops.

As breath travels through us, we can "ride" it inward to the core of who we are. Our inward reception and acceptance of the breath is the Christian acceptance of the Spirit in the breath, in a dimension of breath practice proceeding beyond the intentional breath meditation. We give ourselves over to the Spirit.

Our acceptance of an inner meaning of the breath allows us to abandon images and thoughts in the awareness of being led to our heart. Synergy with the Spirit Breath carries us to an inwardness, the truth of who we are and communion in God Trinity.

Synergy with the Spirit to Trinitarian inwardness is the distinctive Christian character of breathing practice. Actually, this concept of inwardness is the familiar and well-established "indwelling" of the Holy Spirit and the whole Trinity, according to the thirteenth-century Franciscan theologian St. Bonaventure, among others.

Our breath practice uses the intellect for the enlightened awareness of sacred doctrine almost as flashes during the practice, but not as a process of reasoning during the practice; we don't think our way to the heart.

The Spirit finds paths to the heart for each of us who are open; intentional use of the breath in the well-ordered human person can dispose us for internal recollection by and for the Spirit.

Simple expressions, such as being "in the Spirit," can have the most power and significance. St. Paul speaks of the peace arising in the faith relationship with God; life in faith and confidence in hope is effective "because God's love has been poured into our hearts through the Holy Spirit that has been given to us" (Rom 5:5).

Writing in the fourth century, St. Basil the Great states directly: "Through the Spirit we become intimate with God," and he follows with a citation of Galatians 4:6, "And because you are children, God has sent the Spirit of his Son into our hearts, crying, 'Abba! Father!'"[9] As Beloved in the Beloved, we can appreciate God-for-us, breathing the Breath of life and love into our hearts, and allowing us to ride it inward, that we might enter into a relationship with the Father that Jesus opens in the heart of the Trinity, abiding from forever in our hearts.

An obstacle to appreciating the Spirit for our lived integrated spirituality might arise for English-speaking persons, as Holy Spirit was translated from *Spiritus Sanctus* in Latin, "spirit," and in German *geist*, which gave us "Holy Ghost." "Ghost" had an inadvertent but powerful way of removing the Spirit from everydayness!

A wealth of images and words used in Scripture and our early theological ancestors are dynamic, as the Spirit cannot be defined by one analogy and is inherently active. A helpful list was developed by Yves Congar:

Breath, air, wind: this is the very name of the Spirit.

Water, and especially living water.

Fire, tongues of fire (Acts 2:3; Is 6:6) [quoting J. Guillet]: "The great symbols of the Spirit—water, fire, air, and wind—belong to the world of nature and do not have definite shapes; above all they call to mind the idea of being invaded by a presence and of a deep and irresistible expansion."

Dove. [Congar refers to another section of his book for elaboration.]

Anointing, chrism.

Finger of God: ... the instrument and sign of God's power ... and creative power....

Seal: the Spirit with whom the Father anointed Christ at his baptism.... This "seal" represents something final and definitive. The Spirit is the Promised One, the eschatological Gift. In God, he is the fulfillment of the communication of the deity. Athanasius said that the seal that marks us can only be the Spirit, God himself.

> *Love:* see Thomas Aquinas (*C. Gent.* IV, 19; *ST* Ia, q. 37 and parallel texts).
>
> *Gift:* [Congar writes: "this title is so important" that he has devoted a chapter to it in his book. He refers to a chapter on Augustine that will follow; see also Thomas Aquinas *ST* Ia, q. 38 and parallel texts, and Bonaventure.]
>
> *Peace:* see Jn 20:19, 21; cf. verses 22–23; see also Rom 14: 17: "peace and joy in the Holy Spirit."
>
> To these images can be added those used in the liturgy.[10]

Congar is a theologian's theologian who turned to Scripture as foundational and sustained conversation with theological ancestors over the centuries in the Orthodox and Western traditions, for the sake of the faith experience of his contemporaries. He gave the last decades of his life, beginning with his crucial theological expertise in the Second Vatican Council, to the theology of the Holy Spirit.

Congar recognized that Trinitarian theology may be more stated than actually practiced, with more of our attention devoted to Christology. He practiced a profound Trinitarian depth and applied awareness of Irenaeus' two hands of God, with appreciation of the two missions of Word and Breath.

Congar repeated his encouragement, which could also be his epitaph: "No Christology without Pneumatology, and no Pneumatology without Christology."

"Breath," Congar writes, is simply the name of the Spirit. Have we forgotten or never heard this name?

The Spirit is a force, a power, but not an impersonal one. Congar brings a real sensitivity to the personality of the Spirit, who, he writes, is "certainly revealed without a personal face. The Incarnate Word has a face—he has expressed his personality in our human history in the way persons do, and the Father has revealed himself in him. The Spirit does not present such personal characteristics. He is, as it were, buried in the work of the Father and the Son, which he completes."[11]

Congar suggests a self-emptying or *kenosis* of the Spirit, in the Spirit's work, citing recent Orthodox theologians Vladimir Lossky and Paul Evdokimov. "This is why those who have written about the Holy Spirit have frequently called him the 'unknown' or the 'half-known' one. Already in his own time, Augustine noted that the Holy Spirit had never been discussed and his mystery had not been examined."[12]

Congar cites J.R. Villalón in a way that is so close to the heart of our work: "We do not usually spend too much time thinking about the breath that supports the word."[13] And so we turn to the Breath.

Intentionally turning to the Spirit, the unknown or half-known, the two missions of Word and Breath ask us to receive both. The Word reveals the Father and the Father's reign, so that we enter into the Belovedness of the Word. The Spirit reveals in an ongoing way to illumine the hearts of all persons of goodwill and, as seal, is responsible for the life of the Church and the world unto the consummation of time into eternity. The future-oriented final section of the Creed immediately follows the proclamation of the Spirit.

My hope is for our return to awareness or enlightenment that the Spirit is not distant but within each breath the invitation. The Indian poet Kabir, influenced by both the Islamic and Hindu traditions, wrote that God is "the breath within the breath." As Christians our moment of enlightenment is the breakdown of separation of the Spirit from ourselves to a lived unity, a non-duality in the moment. Living within this moment, we are united within God's action and life, and God is not so much within our breath as we are in God's Breath.

The Spirit Working in the Gifts and Fruit and Ongoing Inclinations

Awareness of the activity of the Spirit is far from an innovation in the life of the Church. If it seems so, the current state is a signal of departure from our tradition. Rereading the Acts of the Apostles and the narrative of the earliest days of the post-resurrection community, the Spirit has clearly taken the central role promised by Jesus, that a new advocate would be given.

Paracletos in Greek and *advocatus* in Latin refer to one who has been called to come near to support. And signs of the Spirit's presence and activity are rampant in accounts after Jesus' resurrection and

Pentecost. The medievals, such as Thomas Aquinas and Bonaventure, continued this tradition in their work of synthesis. Their style was that of those who went before them and is the manner of theological reflection in Eastern Christianity: foundation in Scripture and recognition of the guidance of the Spirit in theological reflection over the centuries. That is why they cite the ancestors so often; it is a healthy Christian instinct to see ourselves in the flow of nurturing tradition for active engagement to preserve the faith experience.

Gift and Love were the principal titles of the Spirit for Bonaventure, Aquinas, and other medievals. The Spirit is gift and bears gifts for integrated human response and development, but the bestowal of the Spirit personally is Gift, pure and simple. The dynamic presence of the Spirit of Love was such that some theologians, including the Franciscan school, argued that where one finds love, one finds the Spirit personally. Others argued differently, that love may not be the Spirit personally, but love is caused by the Spirit. For most of the Christian centuries, the Spirit was not "a ghost" and was not "out there," but was linked as cause to love and goodness in the world, and moving through human persons.

In a similar way, significant attention was devoted to the Gifts and Fruit of the Spirit, seen as a means to human actualization and the manifestation of it. Schnackenburg presents the theology of St. John's Gospel and the Spirit as "the principle of life (cf. Jn. 3.5–8; 6.63; 7.38f.)" and the Spirit who "serves Jesus' revelation in his role as Witness and Interpreter (14.26; 15.26; 16.13f.)."[14]

As Interpreter, the Spirit is the new advocate given to remain in the people of God, mystical body of Christ, the Church—our ongoing guide. Pauline theology accords with its eschatological orientation. The ministry of Jesus initiates the reign of God toward the final stage of consummation; we are living in the middle stage, oriented in faith, hope, and love, the Spirit-initiated theological or God-oriented virtues, to that Omega point.[15]

As the Spirit is given to us for this time, the Spirit abides, sustaining us with the Breath and gift of life, which in its full meaning is Trinitarian participation as Beloved. Belovedness includes entry into the very life of God and is grounded in 2 Peter 1:4, that we "may become partakers of the divine nature," prompting the earliest theological reflection on the truly surprising invitation of God to enter the divine life. Effected in each moment, our divinization or *theosis* is a foundational part of Christian self-understanding.

Our *theosis* will be fully actualized in eternity; hence the longing of our hoping faith relationship. It is achieved by the gentle and dynamic power of the Spirit, present in all places and filling all things. Our response is the only condition placed on it. Over the centuries, Christian theologians have recognized the patience of the Spirit with us—patience accompanied by nudges, as gifts are given to us for our response, in our uniqueness and woundedness.[16]

Isaiah 11:1–3 presents the qualities of the future Anointed One in the future era of right relationship and peace that follows from it. The gifts given in Isaiah were later interpreted as gifts given by the Spirit in a particular and unique way to Jesus to fulfill the words of the prophet, but were also given to those incorporated into Christ, for their flourishing. These few words inspired reflection on the activity of the Spirit: "A shoot shall come out from the stock of Jesse, and a branch shall grow out of his roots. The spirit of the LORD shall rest upon him, the spirit of wisdom and understanding, the spirit of counsel and might, the spirit of knowledge and the fear of the LORD, His delight shall be in the fear of the LORD."

St. Gregory the Great (+604; Benedictine monk and later pope) commented on the gifts of the Holy Spirit, and eleventh-century theologians such as Stephen Langton accelerated theological reflection. A century later, St. Thomas Aquinas devoted extensive commentary to the gifts for the sake of understanding and recognizing the action of the Spirit. Medieval theology had an intense belief in the activity of the Spirit.

The gifts narrated in Isaiah are seven: wisdom, understanding, counsel, knowledge, reverence/piety, fortitude, and awe/fear of the Lord. The gifts should be seen as dynamic, to actualize us, rather than as possessions. *Wisdom* can be received in the moment as enlightenment, seeing the big picture, contemplative gaze, mystical apprehension. St. Thomas associated wisdom with the greatest virtue: love. *Understanding*, as a serene insight, can flow from wisdom or contribute to it. *Knowledge* is the moment of reasoning's accomplishment. The medieval hierarchy places wisdom and understanding as comprehensive, above the struggles of rational knowledge. Knowledge gained laboriously over time can be crowned by the Spirit in understanding and wisdom. *Counsel* is the Spirit's inner movement to relationality and good action.

Some medieval writers saw the previous four as gifts of the intellect, which they interpreted broadly to include the heart. They did not segregate the mind from the heart, as has been the case in philosophy in recent centuries. The remaining three gifts were sometimes related to the appetite or will. *Fortitude*, or courage, is a gift to fulfill good counsel and complete the vision of the good action or relationship. *Reverence/piety* and *awe/fear of the Lord* ensure that the human relationship of faith retains its fundamental relationship to God Trinity. Awe can be rediscovered as a gift to naturally accompany wisdom; it prompts praise and gratitude.

An old expression of Western theology is that the human person is *theologal*, that is, fundamentally related to God—a way to connect with the Christological anthropology of Colossians and Ephesians hymns. There may be an advantage in using *reverence* for piety, which meant, in the classical era, the reverence given by a son or daughter of any age to a parent. *Awe* in the face of God Trinity and God's saving work, again, the Ephesians and Colossians hymns can be recalled. Awe summons us to respect the insight of wisdom and to reverence God in action, which sometimes will require self-control, with fortitude, to respect God's reign, way, and teaching—a holy, respectful, and loving awe.

I suggest that a good way to appreciate the Gifts is to memorize them and regularly recite them in our heart; it is not a difficult task. Remembering helps us to integrate and states its importance to us. Remembering God's work invites me to rest and recall the work of the Spirit: *the Spirit empowers me and my sisters and brothers with wisdom ... understanding ... good counsel ... and knowledge ... reverence ... fortitude ... and awe in our loving God Trinity*. Remembering and recalling can support our recognition of God's ever-present work in humanity. The human person is by nature open to God's movement; there is no fundamental divide between grace and nature for St. Thomas. The classical Christian vision of the human person is a beautiful one.

Thus, God works in all persons. Our medieval theological ancestors found a certain prominence for the work of the Spirit in believers who have the Spirit's indwelling in sacramental baptism and the life of grace/vibrant relationship in God. However, they will never limit the power of the Spirit in God's creation.

After St. Thomas addresses the Gifts of the Spirit in the *Summa Theologiae*, he turns to the Beatitudes and the Fruits of the Spirit as guides and manifestations of the Spirit in our lives. The Gifts facilitate response to the movements of the Spirit and the theological virtues of faith relationship, hope, and love; the Beatitudes are guides along the way, and the Fruits are manifestations of our relationship and response.

St. Thomas developed a correlation of the Gifts, Beatitudes, and Fruits, not for the sake of analysis so much as to help the reader enter into the life of the Spirit, with an appreciation of the deep weaving of aspects of life, to give ourselves over to the Spirit. And such is the hope for us, to touch some foundational elements of sacred doctrine for points of awareness in our prayer practice and life of response.

Ours is the challenge to practically shift our awareness of the Spirit's action from the remote and distant sense—to shift from the "out-there" of the Spirit—and to have awareness of the Spirit acting in ourselves and others; to receive the Spirit's animation. Awareness can help us overcome our tendency to self-rejection; we actually are the Beloved. At times we may find hints of the Spirit's action in others before finding it in ourselves. St. Thomas was quite forthright in his localization of the Spirit's action within us. To be honest, can't Thomas help us shift from our default external placement of God?

Karl Rahner wrote in the first volume of his *Theological Investigations* that the very point of contemporary theology had to be the shift from the extrinsicism of God to an internal encounter and response. The very meaning of humanity for Rahner is openness to God and completion or consummation in God in eternity. Rahner tried to recover the dynamic relationality of early theology and the teaching of St. Thomas.

And as the Spirit is a force powerful and gentle, in the words of Eastern Orthodox theology, expect to see initiatives of the Spirit in persons who are well disposed in faith's relationship of docility and obedience to love in action. In Western theology, St. Thomas, as theologian and mystical theologian, frequently and naturally wrote that the Spirit inclines or disposes us for response, the Spirit acting as an inner impulse to actions in love.

So significant is the Spirit in St. Thomas that he describes the New Law of Christ as, first of all, the presence of the Holy Spirit in our hearts, and second, a written law. He cites Jeremiah 31:31–33, cited in Hebrews 8:10, that the law will be written on the hearts of the people as having great authority.

Thomas uses an analogy from Aristotle, that something is known from what is principal or most powerful in it. He uses this for a critical statement about the New Law itself. Thomas writes, "What is most powerful in the law of the New Testament, and in what its strength consists, is the gift of the Holy Spirit, given through faith in Christ."[17]

The Spirit looks for our reception in the living faith relationship as the basis for action in us. We will keep "response" in mind, which is our next section, as we briefly continue with the phenomenon of "reception." Reception in faith should be seen as Trinitarian. Reception of Christ is reception of the Spirit and the Father, as the Trinity is always united. We also know that our reception should not be limited to the intellectual assent, as significant as that is. The Spirit within us looks for a living relationship. Intellectual assent alone might put us in the role of spectators. Prayer awareness of the loving action of the Spirit disposes us to be participants.

How might the inner action of God, given the limits of words, be described? Dominican Sister Mary Ann Fatula is a theologian and mystic. She is born a member of an Eastern Church in union with the Catholic Church, and a member of a Latin Rite religious order; her writing interweaves the wisdom of East and West, emphasizing the centrality of God Trinity. Sister Mary Ann follows both a lived Eastern Trinitarian spirituality and St. Thomas' devotion to practical Trinitarianism, and so emphasizes theology as expressed for the sake of faithful teaching and actualization in our life and experience.

> In the Holy Spirit we receive the very person of infinite love between Father and Son. The Spirit is their embrace, their kiss, their joy and delight lavished upon the world.... Every image [of the Spirit] can only hint at the Spirit's depths as third divine person: powerfully and gently present among and within us as the very heart of God, bestowed upon us now as the completion which all of the symbols promise, given now as the pledge of our final possession (2 Cor 5:5), and, at the end, lavished upon us as our last and infinitely extravagant fulfillment.

> The third divine person's name as Spirit itself connotes the breath and sigh of infinite love between Jesus and his Abba. Because love is the very source and cause of every other gift we bestow, the Spirit's name is not only "Love" but also "Gift." "You shall receive the gift of the Holy Spirit" (Acts 2:38). But this gift is offered to us so that it may truly be ours in an unreturnable bestowal. Thus the Holy Spirit is not only our Abba's Spirit, not only Jesus' Spirit, but truly *our* Spirit as well....[18]

"God's self-bestowal" as God's gift of Self to us is an expression often used by Karl Rahner to describe *charis* (Greek), *gratia* (Latin), or grace. "Grace" is not a thing or commodity, but God's self-giving, God's power, God's love. And the bestowal of the Spirit as our spirit in a unique way seals our unity in God Trinity, as sons and daughters. Rahner would also repeat his profound mystic insight: "Giver and gift are one." What more can God give than God's self through the missions of the Word and the Breath?

Sister Fatula writes with a soul enlightened in loving gratitude to the innermost reality of who we are, communion in the Holy Trinity. As we close this section and turn to the last foundational consideration, "Respond," Sister positions us well in internal abiding in God:

> Our human destiny is not that of isolated egos turned inward but rather of autonomous persons so inwardly secure that we freely turn outward to communion with others. As the very person of love at the heart of God, the Holy Spirit gently and strongly attracts us, healing our wounded wills and freeing us for generous self-giving. Mystics such as Catherine of Siena have so experienced the Spirit filling their hearts that they have seen in the Holy Spirit our mother, nursing us with the infinite gift-love at the heart of God. And this gift-love, agape, is not simply the effect of the Spirit's working us but mysteriously a created participation in the very person of the Holy Spirit.[19]

Abiding within God Trinity doesn't isolate us as individuals; instead, it places us in a point of communion that somehow is also a circle encompassing all creation and all persons.

Notes

1. John of Damascus, *The Fathers of the Church: The Writings of John of Damascus*, trans. Frederic H. Chase (New York: Paulist Press, 1958), 166.
2. Ibid., 167.
3. Yves Congar, OP, *I Believe in the Holy Spirit*, Volume III: *The River of Life Flows in the East and in the West*, trans. David Smith (New York: Seabury Press, 1983), 148. Congar's contribution to the theology of the Spirit, by bringing the wealth of reflection of the centuries to us, is enormous. His three-volume principal work, *I Believe in the Holy Spirit*, was reprinted (New York: Herder & Herder, 2004) in one volume, with the same pagination as the earlier English translation. His *The Word and the Spirit*, trans. David Smith (London: Geoffrey Chapman & San Francisco: Harper & Row, 1986), specifically considers the missions of the Word and the Breath. More recently, a collection of some articles has become available: Yves Congar, OP, *The Spirit of God: Short Writings on the Holy Spirit*, ed. Susan Mader Brown, Mark E. Ginter, Joseph G. Mueller, SJ, and Catherine E. Clifford (Washington, DC: Catholic University of America Press, 2018). Congar suffered many infirmities in his last decades and remained steadfast in his commitment to writing on life in the Word and the Breath. In recognition of his theological contributions, he was named a cardinal of the Catholic Church.
4. *I Believe in the Holy Spirit*, Volume III, 19.
5. Jennifer K. Berensen, Notes to "The Letter of Paul to the Ephesians," in *The New Oxford Annotated Bible*, 4th ed., New Revised Standard Version (New York: Oxford, 2010), 1671.
6. Henri J.M. Nouwen, with Philip Roderick, *Beloved: Henri Nouwen in Conversation* (Grand Rapids, MI, and Cambridge, UK: William B. Eerdmans, 2007). A charm of the book is the inclusion of a CD recording of the conversation on which the book is based: a conversation about Belovedness, an important theme in Nouwen.
7. Henri J.M. Nouwen, *Life of the Beloved* (New York: Crossroad, 2014), 29–30.
8. Ibid., 30.
9. St. Basil the Great, *On the Holy Spirit*, trans. David Anderson (Crestwood, NY: St. Vladimir's Seminary Press, 2011), Sec. 49, 77.
10. Congar, *I Believe in the Holy Spirit*, Volume III, 4–5.
11. Ibid., 5.
12. Ibid.
13. Ibid.
14. Rudolf Schnackenburg, *New Testament Theology Today*, trans. David Askew (Montreal: Palm Publishers, 1963), 96–97.

15 Ibid., 88.

16 Touch, prompt based on an interior word, or even nudge might be suitable terms among so many others. Congar wrote: "C'est une touche, une disposition …," "It is a touch, a disposition…." Yves Congar, *La Parole et Le Souffle* (Paris: Desclée, 1984). It is interesting to note that the French title would be literally translated "The Word and The Breath" but was published in English as *The Word and The Spirit*. Perhaps Congar wanted to make a statement about the collaborative unity of Word and Breath!

17 St. Thomas Aquinas, *Summa Theologiae, I–II, 106, 1, responsio*, my translation.

18 Mary Ann Fatula, OP, *The Triune God of Christian Faith* (Collegeville, MN: Michael Glazier, Liturgical Press, 1990), 93–94.

19 Ibid., 94–95.

CHAPTER 3

Respond

GOD TRINITY IS REVEALED in 1 John 4:8 as *agape*, that sharing, inviting, responding, intermingling, and interpenetrating love that early theology called *perichoresis*. Remarkably, we are foreknown and chosen from all eternity in the Beloved for response and relationship in Jesus and the Spirit as Beloved. Trinitarian inviting and responding love is at the core of who we are as Beloved. Inviting and responding love is our anthropology and foundation for human development, our spirituality, and our moral theology as well.

Thus, inviting and responding love is at the core of our prayer—that is, within our relationship with God Trinity, and in our relations with our brothers and sisters.

My summary proposal for the Christian moral or ethical life might be: "Response in love to God's received initiative of love as well as sharing, inviting, and responding love to our sisters and brothers. We are actualized in Christ Jesus and the unity and power of the Holy Spirit to organically grow into our call as Beloved and divinized unto our final consummation." In this is our truth, actualization, freedom, and flourishing.

I believe this is consistent with Scripture and the theological tradition of the Church. Our ancestor, the great Rabbi Hillel, taught that the summary of the Law is love of God and neighbor; everything else is commentary. All norms and asceticism are only meaningful within the dynamic of love, a love that God has initiated before the first moment of time.

Our prayer practice is a response to God's initiative for union. Our pattern is in breathing, receiving the meaning of God's Breath and Beloved, and response by giving ourselves over to God's self-bestowal in the outbreath. Our life in the cosmos and with our brothers and sisters is all a consequence of God's love. A spiritual father (or director) once blessed me with the expression "May you be a consequence of God's charity." Amen. Love throughout its spectrum is indivisible, prompted by God's Breath, the Spirit of Love.

Response is a culmination of the Christian life in God, because the Good News of God's vision of creation of the human is for loving, just, and thus peaceful relationships in God Trinity, among ourselves with our brothers and sisters, and toward the earth itself.

Judaism and Christianity understood themselves as religions of response. From God's initiative to Moses in Mt. Sinai to Jesus' invitation to abide within Trinitarian love, stage after stage of revelation begins with God's initiative to invite response in relationship. In classical Catholic theology, the human person was seen as having a nature (which is a gift from God) that is intrinsically open to encounter with God (the gift of God's self, or supernatural). One Latin term is that the human person possesses *capax dei*, or the capacity for God; another is *potentia obedientialis*, the potential for obediential response to God. Both are ancient and significant, and carry the sense of the exalted dignity of humanity.

Salvation history is one of ongoing relational invitation, which continues now unto consummation. A robust Christian anthropology confronts an empirical cultural reductionist default of humanity's solely biological, sociological, or consumerist identity.

Nor should we accept a defeatist understanding of humanity and an over-emphasis on sin, or an extrinsic and legalistic type of "grace" that overlooks the Scriptural and lived classical understanding of invitation to internal relationship. Perhaps an ancient confidence in God's steadfast relationality is the basis for the permanent persistence of the contemplative tradition within the ancient churches of Eastern Orthodoxy and Catholicism.

As Trinity is the core and most important Christian doctrine, indicating an unknowable relationality of love, response is one of relational love. "God is love"; *ho theos agape estin*, that God is a sharing love (1 John 4:8). Human persons are within the loving orbit of Trinitarian love, extending out and drawing close: a centripetal and centrifugal love encompassing us and the fate of the cosmos.

Love's inwardness/outwardness invites distinctions but not separations. We will first address the phenomenon of response to God; then to loving response in and to God Trinity; and finally to response to God, that is also response to other persons in community.

The Phenomenon of Response

We have noted that Judaism and Christianity are religions of relationship and response. "Receive" and "Respond" have a vital link and are interwoven in relationship. The awareness of reception prompts the love of gratitude for the gift of love as well as response to the giver. Rahner's insight that "Giver and Gift are one" invites continued reflection. For me, his simple statement has been so powerful a force for recognition in moments over the decades. We are immersed in God, and God is not separate from God's self-gift!

A foremost American Protestant theologian of the twentieth century, H. Richard Niebuhr, in *The Responsible Self* (1963), initiated substantial contemporary discussion on response as foundational to the meaning of human life and the basis for the Christian moral life. German theologian Bernard Häring was the foremost Catholic moral theologian of the twentieth century. He positioned response as the key element and leitmotif of Christian ethics in his trilogy *Free and Faithful in Christ* (1978)—response to God and to our sisters and brothers.[1] I propose reception as the spiritual basis for response, both within the Spirit of God.

Häring incorporated biblical and virtue ethics in a renewed spirit within the energy of relationality, for vigilant, free, faithful, and authentic living. His earlier *The Law of Christ* (1959) was a prompt for the next stage of renewal for Catholic moral theology. Häring was cited as a critical influence by Gerard Gilleman in *The Primacy of Charity in Moral Theology*. Gilleman crafted an explicit advocacy of the centrality of love, following Scripture and St. Thomas Aquinas, in a dynamic representation of the tradition.[2]

Formulations of the Eastern Church and the Western Church have unique histories regarding their liturgical expressions, reflecting the significance of their history and experience; Congar finds a common Trinitarian dynamic. It is intended for us to recognize and enter, and live in our everyday experience of our divine relationship and identity:

> Although there were great differences between the liturgy of the East and that of the West both in form and in expression, the reality and genius underlying them were, at the deepest level, the same. In both, the liturgy was a celebration of the "mystery".... The whole of the liturgy expresses and brings about a movement of God towards us and of us towards God. The movement passes from the Father through the Son in the Spirit and returns in the Spirit through the Son to the glory of the Father, who takes us, as his children, into communion with him. The Spirit is therefore invoked in every liturgical action, to be active and present in the liturgy.[3]

"From the Father through the Son in the Spirit" is the first movement of invitation for reception, and the second movement, our response, "returns in the Spirit through the Son to the glory of the Father, who takes us, as his children, into communion with him." To use a spatial analogy, the movements might be likened to a swooping down and a gathering upward. While the analogy would honor God's transcendence, it could risk falling into an up-there and isolated God. Perhaps more effective could be the analogy of a spiritual centrifugal movement of God Trinity, to reference the coming-from, and then a centripal movement of gathering to communion. St. Thomas Aquinas taught this dual movement, the *exitus-reditus*, or going out from and returning to God.

Reception-Response is an image of the inner life of the Trinity and is expressed for us, the missions of the Word and Breath, the two hands of God, in the unforgettable words of St. Irenaeus.

In the Son, In the Spirit

Word and Breath are active for us; they bring us to our identity as Beloved in the Beloved and bring us back, over and over in our lives. The two hands are ever present: silent, powerful, and gentle.

"In the Son" deserves attention, as the Son is the template for humanity. Speaking from the Franciscan tradition, Richard Rohr uses it to overcome the distance we place between humanity and God, as if we are an afterthought rather than chosen from all eternity.

We've noted that the simple "in Christ" is a powerful expression for overcoming the extrinsicism given God. Christ Jesus immersed himself in our humanity that we might enter into his divinity and relationship with the Father in the Spirit.

Abiding in Jesus means welcoming other persons into relationship, following Jesus. Romans 15:7 exhorts a key principle of moral theology: "Welcome one another, therefore, just as Christ has welcomed you, for the glory of God." Commenting on Romans, Brendan Byrne writes: "A familiar biblical pattern of motivation is operative here: what one has oneself received from God, one is bound to extend to one's fellow human beings (cf. Deut 24:17–22; Matt 18:32–33)."[4]

Similarly, "in the Spirit" has a unique significance. The Spirit is given to us for the moment and for the future, inviting intentional awareness. We might have icons or religious images strategically placed to remind us of who we are and to renew us in the moment. The face of Christ, of course, particularly invites us, in the icon, to find in his eyes our relationship and to rest in his eyes.

The Spirit is invisible; in the icon tradition of the Eastern Church, one must not attempt a physical rendition of the Spirit or the Father. Yet the Spirit, in the mission from the Father, is "present in all places and filling all things, the treasury of blessings and the giver of life," a most familiar prayer of the Christian East. Thus, invisible but "present in all places" might mean particularly available to us, even in each aware breath.

Justice to the work of the Spirit demands a further consideration. The Creed proclaims the Spirit as "the Lord and Giver of Life." Our extrinsicism will safely locate the Spirit moving over the waters at the beginning of creation, yet life is breathed at every moment; the development of the Church is entrusted to the Spirit by Jesus as another advocate in Pentecost, and the Spirit will sustain the path of the cosmos unto consummation in Trinitarian communion. Belief and reliance on the nudging and consummating work of the Spirit gives a deep confidence in the stronger current below the surface waters and their risks.

In what way does the Spirit sustain us? We noted earlier the attention given to the Spirit's action by our medieval theological ancestors. They used words such as *inclinatus* to witness how the Spirit inclines or moves us to action; in contemporary English, we could just as easily say the Spirit nudges our hearts to awareness, attitudes, and action. We can just as easily use contemporary speech, true to the tradition, that humanity is the Spirit's zone of ongoing dedicated activity.

Over the centuries the theological virtues of faith, hope, and love; the Gifts of the Spirit (Isa 11:2); and the Fruits of the Spirit (Gal 5:22) were called out as the Spirit's contemporaneous action. The Beatitudes are presented as a manner in which the Spirit sustains us in the likeness of Jesus, whom tradition identifies as the prime analog and fulfillment of the Beatitudes. Our second part places them in the context of practice.

Oriented to Practice

Again, the purpose of our reflection on response is not for demonstration, but for practical theological awareness in prayer. We are persons of reception and response. Continued practice and docility to the Spirit makes us increasingly attentive to God's sharing and relational love as we read or hear Scripture, in the Sacraments and most of all for the present moment of reception and response.

Ongoing moments are opportunities for the Spirit to cultivate us for insight in prayer and rest in prayer. Over time, response becomes more integrated within us. Like the hesychasts of Orthodoxy, Blessed John Ruusbroec frequently repeated the significance of prayer as rest. Response to God is active in attentiveness prayer and in turning from destructive practices to growth and flourishing in virtue, integrating us and leading to an active rest within response. Life in the Spirit takes apart separations like action and rest; they are integrated by the Spirit!

When we pray, we do so abiding in the mystical and pancosmic body of Christ, animated by the Spirit, with the living legacy of wisdom given by the Spirit over the centuries. The Christian is relational in the moment yet aware of the lived centuries of love by our ancestors in God Trinity.

As rest can accompany response to God, arising from reception of God's love, reception supports our return to self in a self-remembering that can be a bridge from reception to response. We come back to ourselves and in doing so are now more free for response.

The parable of the Prodigal Son (Luke 15:11–32) has a wonderful moment when the young man who has squandered his inheritance is far off and bereft, tending pigs as a hired hand. He had demanded his share of inheritance and gone off, isolated from his father, brother, and homeland. At some point in his anguish, perhaps even prompted by hunger, verse 17 relates that "he came to himself."

"He came to himself" has been a most powerful line of Scripture for me over the years. Coming back to myself can be difficult in times of anguish, when one can be seemingly enclosed by adversity. Self-recovery in anguish requires a deep-seated awareness that requires cultivation.

The young man of the parable had a breakthrough moment. He finally recalled, and there was drama in Jesus' narrative, that he had severed his relationship with his father but that he might be able to renew something of it. On a deep level he may have recalled his father's relationality. Faith is relationship and reliance and is manifested in hope. The young man overcame the distance he had created and set off with a repentance he had not experienced until his crisis. His father's response was true to abiding relationship in welcoming and accepting love.

We also recall the elder brother who remained home in fidelity and his protest to his father's warm welcome. Yet the young man is beloved. It was a prompt for their father to repeat what he had said earlier (v. 24, then v. 32 to close the parable): "he was dead and has come to life; he was lost and has been found." He was lost and has been dead to communion, lost in his self-imposed exile to himself and in his isolation.

Years ago, a professor of poetry taught me the benefit of this coming to ourselves. He called it self-remembering, and I applied it first to my own identity and then to my awareness of falling short in relationality. Turning to the Gospel passage, "he came to himself" became linked with "self-remembering" and self-recovery. Self-remembering has real meaning in our ongoing conversion process. It is, I believe, our work for each moment of encounter, to relate and remember ourselves and others as love, present to ourselves and God Trinity.

This, I propose, is also the work and fruit of the breathe-receive-respond practice. As this foundations part closes, it is my hope that by receiving, first, Breath as Spirit and love, and then receiving the Beloved and our identity as Beloved in the Beloved, we will respond in loving self-recovery of our identity in God Trinity, who is available in each aware breath and for accepting encounter of our brothers and sisters.

Notes

1   H. Richard Niebuhr, *The Responsible Self: An Essay in Christian Moral Philosophy* (Louisville, KY: Westminster John Knox Press, 1999); Bernard Häring, *Free and Faithful in Christ: Moral Theology for Priests and Laity* (Middlegreen, Slough: St. Paul Press, 1978). Häring's stress on response within moral theology has been formational to me. As Christian ethics has engaged philosophical insights into the human person over the centuries, Häring turned to insights of developmental psychology for discourse on human flourishing. A most helpful resource for Christian ethics is the volume *Character Strengths and Virtues: A Handbook and Classification*, by Christopher Peterson, PhD, & Martin E.P. Seligman, PhD (Washington, DC: American Psychological Association; New York: Oxford University Press, 2004).

2   Bernard Häring, *The Law of Christ: Moral Theology for Priests and Laity*, trans. Edwin G. Kaiser, CPPS (Cork: Mercier Press, 1967); Gerard Gilleman, SJ, *The Primacy of Charity in Moral Theology*, trans. William F. Ryan, SJ, and Andre Vachon, SJ (London: Burns & Oates, 1959).

3   Yves M.J. Congar, *I Believe in the Holy Spirit*, Vol. I: *The Holy Spirit in the "Economy," Revelation and Experience of the Spirit*, trans. David Smith (New York: Seabury, 1983), 104.

4   Brendan Byrne, SJ, *Romans* (Collegeville, MN: Michael Glazier, Liturgical Press, 2007), 429.

PART II

Practice

CHAPTER 1

Breathing

That we are incorporated as Beloved in the Beloved into the very life of God Trinity is a most astonishing statement of our tradition, and thus our Christian life is anything but static.

When we are willing to enter a dynamic vision of the faith, images such as the double movement from St. Thomas, the *exitus-reditus*, or going forth and returning of Jesus' incarnation and return with creation to God the Father; and the classic formula with the same spirit cited by Congar, "from the Father, in the Son, through the Spirit, and then in the Spirit, through the Son, to the Father" become more robust. The more contemporary image of centrifugal (love proceeding) and centripetal (love gathering) can open a path out of a static or abstract Christianity based on a God who is safely "out there."

Life's grand dynamic is Trinitarian life, and we are a part of it. Because the sacred authors of Genesis used the image of God breathing into soil and animating it, then God's own breath, God's intimacy, is at the heart of humanity as God's radical presence to all.

Humanity's breath as bestowed by God and experienced by ourselves is exactly my starting point for prayer practice. I believe God offers us reception of our breath as a gift of present and intimate love. Our intentional and aware inhalation is acceptance of love in our moment and anywhere. We repeat the practice to grow in the quiet prayer of the heart (*hesychia*) in communion with the Word and Breath, toward communion in the Father. Our practice can be foundational for a path of contemplative living.

Earlier we proposed that the word *pneuma, ruah,* breath is polyvalent; the word has multiple powers. "Polyvalent" evokes powers rather than meanings. In theological writing, we have tended to emphasize "spirit," but the biblical "breath, wind" is gaining appreciation. Congar retrieves from Scripture and tradition that Breath is simply the name of the Spirit of God.

When we breathe intentionally, we create the possibility of, over time, breathing meditatively, first for breath awareness, peace, and recollection, and then, uniquely Christian, to breathe with God intimate to our breath, and to quiet prayer of the heart and rest in God Trinity as Beloved in the Beloved. Our breath may be something we take for granted and see as a mechanical biological process. Entering the polyvalence of breath gives us the alternative of receiving it as God's animating breath of life and love.

The natural start is revisiting breathing itself as an experience. We might tend to breathe in a more shallow than deeper manner. Of course, we become wrapped up in things, and activities that are very engaging bring us into what Csikszentmihalyi identifies as "flow experience."[1] To be in the flow can be very positive and signifies engagement. The daily work of loving interactions brings us into a flow state; we may not even be aware of our bodies, much less our breathing.

Yet beneath it all is our breath, which Genesis gives us as the symbol of God's intimacy with us at creation and in each moment. Hence attention to breathing for entry into the symbol for a deep communion with the Giver of life and love.

We can appreciate love at the in-breath and better respond in love at the out-breath. Receiving is the work of the in-breath, and the in-breath carries openness for the out-breath of loving response. When we breathe intentionally, love is not so much thought of, but rather arises in awareness and leaves before it turns into a thought. Loving presence in communion is the movement rather than thinking about it. Practice in the method doesn't require much in time, but it must be intentional.

For years my appreciation of the breath was primarily an abstract or academic one. Scripture and ancient Christian writers referenced breath as life in its most primal sense. The analogy of prayer to the "breath of the soul" is a gift of the Eastern Church, the more ancient branch of Christianity. What was lacking was a way to translate the growing intellectual awareness to my own life and prayer. At this point, Thich Nhat Hanh, the great Vietnamese Buddhist monk, entered.

Many Christians will sincerely ask what the relationship between this monk and our prayer might be. In the back of their minds, they might fear that a blend or syncretism of belief could be under way. Actually, I had those same concerns years ago.

A first response to reassure and invite might be the reminder about Buddhism, which is not a theological religion; our brothers and sisters have a profound spiritual practice but not a theology, hence there's not a risk of a blend. A second response is in the Catholic tradition: for decades, the Vatican has encouraged conferences of monks from the Catholic and Buddhist traditions to meet and share spiritual practices. A third response is my experience that mid-twentieth-century Catholic monastic exploration of Buddhism first attended to the role of the intellect in Asian and Western meditation and use of the *koan*. With Jesuit William Johnston, breath practice was given more attention. Our study is based on insights in breath meditation practice and awareness. A fourth response is the simple fact of Christianity's history of dialogue with the world's philosophies and religions, recognizing as the Spirit of God leads persons of goodwill to the good, we can be in a world of shared understanding. For hundreds of years, Christianity encountered Greek philosophy and came to use some of its methodology to express itself. And the fifth response, the encounter with Zen practice, can be the occasion, prompted by God's Spirit, I believe, to bring us to another prayer and life practice that is truly Christian, and as offered here, explicitly Trinitarian.

Thich Nhat Hanh studied in Asia and in the United States. He bore a unique witness to peace and nonviolence as well as developing "engaged Buddhism," which evacuated many Vietnamese persons at risk during the war in Vietnam. In his years in the West, he spoke to religiously diverse groups, including many Christians, about living in freedom and compassion. His teaching begins with and is sustained by breath meditation.

Breathing can be done with attention, which requires some thinking at first, with attention the fruit of thinking. Attention can allow integration through our body, mind, and spirit. All of the theological reflection of Part I is for the sake of practice here in Part II and in life. Taking the time to observe and receive our breath is a practical form of asceticism (Greek *acesis* means athletic training) to entirely dispose ourselves to the Spirit.

Breath is for attention, and, over time, attention to breath can have moments of a unique capture of the breath by the Spirit or Breath to bring us to the active rest of love. Love is the attention that accompanies breathing, receives it, and responds at in-breath, quiet possession of breath, and response of out-breath. Very often we may experience continued inwardness at the in-breath; other times the out-breath will take us to loving response in action.

In his little book *How to Sit*, Thich Nhat Hanh writes:

The first thing to do is to stop whatever else you are doing.
Now sit down somewhere comfortable.
Anywhere is fine.
Notice your breathing.
As you breathe in, notice that you are breathing in.
As you breathe out, notice that you are breathing out.[2]

These lines are something of a prelude and introduction to his teaching. My first reading was just prior to sitting in groups to practice mindful breathing. We were Christians in a range of churches, Jewish persons, and persons with no religious affiliation. We experienced a bond of community in the practice and experience of peace and compassion to each other that we promised to sustain beyond our circle. Sitting together is so helpful for guided initial experience. A timer can help when alone; set it for a minute at first, so that you aren't tempted to check progress.

Over time, in my own meditative prayer, a newness and ease arose, renewing my forty years of practice. Animating me was the presence of God to my breathing, God's breath to my breath. A Lutheran pastor with whom I first shared this Christian practice called it "breathing with God."

As I recalled my study of Orthodox prayer, I appreciated the hesychasts who practiced the prayer of stillness and prayer of the heart that unifies all in love. It became more and more real for me, a present reality of love.

To pray with breathing, we first learn to breathe in order to gently and intentionally receive the breath. Upright sitting is a good way to begin. But sit without tension. At first it will be hard to focus on our breathing alone. A suggestion is given to think of nothing but our breath and to count off ten breaths. At first I found this impossible! Humans are made for multiple awareness. After longer than five, ten, or twenty minutes of breathing practice, but not counting, I came to manage great focus at times. Proficiency grows organically; we are coming home to ourselves in breathing. You might remember the ten-count breath exercise and be surprised that the impossible is now natural.

Once you're skilled in breathing practice, you will be able to engage it almost anywhere, in any posture, and at any time; breath and the Spirit are given to us as animating companions.

Your breath meditation becomes your practice, and breath is your companion while walking, sitting, resting before sleep, and before your morning rise. Find yourself where you are and then notice your breath. It might be hurried or shallow. We are not in a rush.

Breathe through your nose, and on your next breaths invite a deeper, gentle descent in your lungs. After several seconds, breathe out gently. Consider building up breath awareness to gain proficiency. Proficiency means that over time, only a few breaths will be needed to reconnect and self-remember.

Breath's deeper descent and return loop reminds us of God's movement of love outward and encompassing for a gathering return. As you gain experience, your breath will not be forced, but you will find it descending even deeper. Some Orthodox hesychasts advocated bowing the beard to the chest during the Jesus Prayer and breathing to an experienced point below the navel. In traditional Chinese medicine and t'ai chi, the *Dantian* or *tan t'ien* is also the area below the navel and a seat of energy; it is a focus for breathing.

Meditating with Thich Nhat Hanh

In the first meditation of *How to Sit*, Thich Nhat Hanh writes that simply sitting "with your mind awake, calm, and clear" takes some training and practice.[3] Here he describes the rapid self-recovery possible as proficiency is developed:

> In our daily lives, our attention is dispersed. Our body is in one place, our breath is ignored, and our mind is wandering. As soon as we pay attention to our breath, as we breathe in, these three things—body, breath, and mind—come together. This can happen in just one or two seconds. You come back to yourself. Your awareness brings these three elements together, and you become fully present in the here and the now. You are taking care of your body, you are taking care of your breath, and you are taking care of your mind.
>
> When you make a soup, you have to add together all the right ingredients in harmony and let them simmer. Our breath is the broth that brings the different elements together. We bathe spirit and mind in our breath and they become integrated so they are one thing. We are whole.
>
> We don't need to control our body, mind, and breath. We can just be there for them. We allow them to be themselves. This is nonviolence.[4]

Cooking is a good analogy, as it takes time. In the same way, breath practice for full awareness of the here and now takes time and, like cooking, patience.

A Christian Engagement with Thich Nhat Hanh

Thich Nhat Hanh identifies Zen practice as "looking deeply" in the moment. In addition to awareness of the moment in breath practice, the practitioner can be aware of self and our attitudes, passions, and impermanence.

Many Christians will identify "meditation" with recollected attention to reading Scripture with pious attention or reflecting on a particular topic. Known as mental prayer or discursive meditation, the venerable, almost thousand-year-old method begins with recollection and progresses to intellectual meditation that intends to culminate in love of God and end in thanksgiving. You can use breathing meditation and invitation of the Holy Spirit as a recollection for the traditional form.

Zen is a particular practice of mindful breathing and awareness for the moment. Perhaps the breath-based method we offer is something of a Christian Zen in the sense of breath integration for the moment.

But breath for my practice is also accompanied by the Holy Spirit, who relates "breathe" to "receive" and "receive" to "respond" for us, and empowers it with the gift of wisdom and theological virtue of love. Our breathing is in God and shaped by the Spirit and the Beloved, to receive, respond, and rest in love.

As he introduces his readers to the meditative practice of awareness, Thich Nhat Hanh writes that meditation is practiced if it is joyous.[5] Yes! Love, joy, and peace are the first fruits of the Holy Spirit. Meditation, contemplation, and prayer integrate mind and heart in communion with God, our source, love, and goal for communion with our brothers and sisters.

Franciscan advocate and teacher of the contemplative tradition Richard Rohr relates—and I can affirm this from personal experience—that when meditation was taught decades ago, most often in religious communities, it was the discursive process usually based on a reading or topic for reflection. While there was always the hope for the affective expression to God, we were often isolated in the intellect, trying to find a way to our heart. Many of us gave up in sadness, struggling with the task of even achieving recollection.

My original hope in practicing Zen breathing meditation was integrated awareness of intellect and heart for recollection in discursive meditation. Such was my intersection of meditation traditions leading to our Christian breathing-in-God practice.

Where can meditation be practiced? Thich Nhat Hanh recognizes that sitting meditation will first come to mind, but it really has no bounds. "Mindfulness meditation can be practiced anywhere and in whatever position the body is in—whether we are sitting, walking, standing or lying down."[6] I concur. Breath practice becomes home for the person for authentic being in the present moment. Mindfulness breath practice is best learned in a comfortable upright sitting position with the back straight and hands placed before us, usually one on each leg, or hands gently folded. As noted earlier, we can use a timer (cell phone timers can be very helpful if meditating alone), employing the breathing practice described just above for varying times. Such is particularly helpful when we're building competency in breathing.

At first it may be just a few breaths with attention given fully to the breath, but we will extend to two and five and ten and twenty minutes of simple breath awareness, eyes closed or soft focus, to build our first foundation of self-presence in the moment. We can use a mindfulness app to gain facility in breathing practice; our Christian breathing practice will be the topic of each section that follows.

Orthodox writers such as the notable Metropolitan Kallistos Ware are emphatic that prayer of heart can be practiced at all times and in all locations and body positions. My first prayer practice is upon waking and before rising, rediscovering the gift of breath, in which awareness of the Holy Spirit emerges. It requires not a thought, but reception of the breath and then Spirit in the breath. These moments after waking can have wonderful clarity and presence. Checking the weather and reviewing work emails can wait for a few moments.

There's always a place of privilege for a more formal, seated posture for practice. Thich Nhat Hanh writes that "A stable posture grounds body and mind"[7] and that wherever we practice, "enjoy your sitting."[8] Being seated in an upright posture becomes natural, and the posture is an invitation to serenity.

In Zen, returning to our breathing is a return home; as a Christian, I find this a happy statement. Christians who are aware of their selves and aware of their relatedness to God Trinity, others, and the world that surrounds them should be the most serene and content persons imaginable. Didn't God create us for this gentle incarnate ease and relationship with Mother Earth?

A walk in the city or park or countryside can be such a moment of grateful joy to the aware Christian: we were made for this moment of ease and peace within and for all.

Unity of the person, dimensions of mind, spirit, and body seem so natural in Christian prayer of the heart, as the heart is the center of the human person; breathing can be the practice of unification for an integrated spirituality.

Thich Nhat Hanh suggests beginning breathing meditation with a gentle smile in the relaxation to begin a sitting meditation: "Sit in such a way that you feel completely at ease. Relax every muscle of your body, including the muscles of your face. The best way to relax the muscles of your face is to smile gently as you breathe in and out."[9]

The meditative smile has an outward expression and inward dimension, an inner smile. It's a gentle, not forced or extreme expression. Thich Nhat Hanh writes: "Your smile relaxes all of your facial muscles. When you smile to your whole body, it is as if you are bathed in a fresh, cool stream of water."[10]

My Christian response is appreciative. It seems natural in Christian prayer, as the opening versicle of liturgy of the hours, or divine office, in the Western Church is: "Lord, open my lips, and my mouth shall proclaim your praise. Glory to the Father and to the Son and to the Holy Spirit...."

If we pray "Lord, open my lips," couldn't a gentle smile of response to God arise? A smile expresses love in the most simple manner, shows our attention, and expresses joy in presence and communion.

Breathing practice as prayer expresses faith. The early biblical theology of faith had a strong dimension of trust and reliance on God. Over the centuries, the intellectual dimension of faith received growing attention; for many, faith is largely intellectual. Breath helps restore the balance and places us in the moment, finding God Trinity's guiding presence in the breath given us.

In the course of the day we are carried into many concerns of our relationships, responsibilities, and interests, with our "flow experience" of connection. When one task is completed, another awaits us. Our breath can call us back to ourselves along the way, and in the words of Dorothy Day, "on the fly."

But what can call us back to our breath? We can use reminders and be creative in it. The mindfulness bell has numerous digital applications, programmable for varying amounts of time. The bell invites us in a breathing self-remembering for the duration of its tone. Often, we simply can't use this type of reminder. A non-digital reminder I use is the small wrist rope version of the Jesus Prayer as a witness to God Trinity's wraparound love; I often miss it and it sometimes surprises me. We might feel a breeze or gust of wind outside. Many other times, in the midst of activities, we will be prompted by our breath itself. Time and practice will do their work of attentiveness and vigilance.

Zen practice hears the bell's sound as an invitation for formal breath meditation. Thich Nhat Hanh describes a process or ritual for inviting the bell's sound, of three breaths prior to the bell.[11] He writes that the bell means a stop, a shift, a return to the moment in the breath: "Ride on the sound of the bell and on your breath to go home to yourself, to go home to the present moment, to the here and the now. You learn the art of being alive, of being present. To be alive means to be in the here and the now so that we can be in touch with the wonders of life within us and around us."[12]

I had already experienced "riding the breath" inward, but Thich Nhat Hanh gave me the words for the music of the breath. He weaves together the flow of breath inward with the way we return to ourselves in self-remembering. At times, it can be a deepening experience in the moment. At other times, it can call us to a shift in perspective, a change of mind, or in the biblical term, *metanoia*.

Responding to the invitation of the Trinity, breath is so linked with the intimacy of the Spirit, the Breath of God, who leads me in, accompanying my riding the breath to ever-present communion with God within ... and to myself, reclaimed in the breath of life. The bell and breath helps in ordinary everyday life to return to myself as the Prodigal Son self-remembered and "came to himself" for a change in perspective and life.

As we continually rediscover the breath in the moments of life, we can be gratefully surprised by it and the creative love of the Breath of God given to us. And the Spirit brings the gifts first expressed in Isaiah 11:2; perhaps in the mindful breath are the gifts of wisdom or enlightenment, which St. Thomas correlates with the greatest theological virtue: love.

The mindful breath can also carry the gift of reverence and awe for the breath and the Breath of God. We might be prompted to invoke the Spirit with the brief, meaningful, and ancient prayer "Come Holy Spirit" at our reception of the breath, not to accompany a physical exercise but because the Spirit as life accompanies the breath as person.

Breathing prayer can lead us to self-review and growth. Our development is a project we share with the Holy Spirit, who gives gifts and helps us bear fruit. Thich Nhat Hanh teaches the important work of seeing ourselves clearly in breathing meditation and "transforming the depths" of our consciousness in honesty and self-compassion.[13] As he applies Buddhist teaching and sutras to his practice, Christians can apply the revelation and wisdom of the Scriptures to our being in the present moment.

Being in the moment with a contemplative everyday awareness can invite specific attention to our attitudes and actions. Might the example of the Prodigal Son come to mind? Have I been mindless in acquisitions? Has this been ongoing? Have I regarded persons in a shallow and transactional manner, rather than accepting and encountering them in their uniqueness? How can I live more authentically in practical ways? Disposing ourselves to the Spirit can lead us forward in renewed life as the Spirit helps us know ourselves and heals and supports our directionality. Self-compassion may be new to us and is critical. God is nothing but kindness and love for us as an emerging Beloved daughter or son. Our kind God invites us to be kind to ourselves.

We might use the pace of the breath for recollection and preparation for an inward structured prayer, such as the fundamental prayer the Lord taught us, "Our Father...." Sometimes I simply repeat inwardly, "Our Father" several times, or "Abba ... Abba" before breathing my way in and entering the prayer.

We can be given, in an inspired moment, other expressions or phrases for our own use. A phrase in my personal use is "I am made in love for love." It came into my awareness in silent breathing prayer and helps me remember myself as I breathe into awareness of self, the Spirit, and the Beloved toward the Father. Usually I recall it once or twice, and it helps me to move along. If I notice an internal movement that doesn't accord with my true identity, I try to pray "Tame me, Holy Spirit."

Breathing for Return to the Moment

A day can be a whirlwind of demands, encounters, or an experience of aloneness even in a crowd. Thich Nhat Hanh shows how breath practice can bring us back to ourselves in the moment. "It takes five or ten seconds for us to restore ourselves fully and produce our true presence in the here and the now."[14] Depending on the moment, it can take longer; we might encounter a situation of sadness or great injustice. Yet we might be able over time to invite ourselves for a pause with awareness of our surrounding demands and concerns, often while beginning the breath practice, to help us engage and invite the Spirit's movement.

Breath practice has an end in itself, which is attentive and wise being-in-the-moment. It is an excellent practical discipline; contemplative prayer is practical as it takes us to the moment in God or with our sisters and brothers. The self-discipline of the early stages yields to an ease, but the trials of life present new challenges to practice. I related my original hope that breath practice would be a more recollected state for traditional intellectual-affective meditation. It gave me that and took me further when I retrieved the Judeo-Christian symbolism of breath.

To me, the gift for Christians is that breath is like Rahner's approach to a symbol: it has meaning in itself and points to more. The pointing beyond itself to greater meaning is what the next section, "Receiving," is about.

"Breathing" and "Receiving" complete each other. Our distinction is to more effectively reunite them.

Notes

1. Mihaly Csikszentmihalyi and Isabella Selega Csikszentmihalyi, eds., *Optimal Experience: Psychological Studies of Flow in Consciousness* (Cambridge, New York, Melbourne: Cambridge University Press, 1995).
2. Thich Nhat Hanh, *How to Sit* (Berkeley, CA: Parallax Press, 2014), 6–9.
3. Ibid., 11.
4. Ibid., 12–13.
5. Ibid., 28.
6. Ibid., 33.
7. Ibid., 42.
8. Ibid., 53.
9. Ibid., 46.
10. Ibid., 50.
11. Ibid., 55.
12. Ibid., 58.
13. Ibid., 79.
14. Ibid., 85.

CHAPTER 2

Receiving

As BREATH IS A polyvalent word with several powers, it is fitting to distinguish the two aspects of "receiving" in prayer practice: learning how to receive the breath, which we've just completed, and receiving the breath taking us to a Trinitarian fullness of relationship.

Breathing becomes receiving, and reception is for response. Breathing is reception of breath for being in the moment in an aware and recollected way, and breathing is discovered as reception of God Trinity, who accompanies your breath for the sake of your inner response in God and response to our brothers, sisters, and Mother Earth.

Breathing becomes receiving, and reception is for response. We have used theological reflection for a foundation, and now in receiving and response, go beyond thought to moments of awareness, prompted by the Spirit.

Receiving the Spirit-Breath of God brings us to awareness of the Word and his reception; our life and theology is Trinitarian. St. Irenaeus coined the wonderful expression of the Word and Spirit as "the two hands of God," and so what could be more natural than to be enfolded in these two hands and arms of communion and oriented to the Father, the Abba of Jesus?

Three typical steps of theological awareness follow: first, awareness of the Spirit with our breathing; followed by awareness and reception of the Word, the Beloved, for awareness; and reception of Abba Father, who is source and goal of communion. Blessed John Ruusbroec describes our entry into contemplative awareness of Trinitarian communion as an active rest, "for God is a flowing

and ebbing sea which ceaselessly flows out into all his beloved...."[1]
He gives a lovely image of the active return of God to us when our prayer gets distracted; another wave of presence and love invites us to return.

The Holy Spirit, Breath of God gives us intimacy in loving presence. It is an intimacy beyond abstraction and reflection. Breathing in God, we are given lived awareness in the Breath and in the Word. The two hands of God bring the depth of our own identity, sharing Belovedness in the Beloved Word and in the active Spirit. We are actualized, for ourselves and response.

Awareness of the Spirit

In our practice, first awareness may be of the Spirit-Breath of God, as we are learning to breathe with receptivity, and then awareness of the Beloved, and a return to the Spirit. We will address these three potential steps, with "awareness" the key term.

Awareness beyond abstraction is known in the Christian East in hesychastic prayer of the heart, and for the Christian West in Blessed John Ruusbroec. Imageless meditation includes the experience of awareness, for those open and disposed to it, for imageless communion. Imageless contemplation should not be put off as inaccessible or dramatic; Blessed John teaches that when established in us, it has an everydayness.

Giving ourselves over to the Spirit can be expressed, over time, by taking the path of the breath within to communion. Recognition of the Spirit's intimacy to my breath doesn't require a lot of thought in the moment, but gratitude for the insight and a further acceptance of the path within.

Study of our sacred texts will dispose us to receive the Spirit in our silent, focused breathing practice. Yet it can't be forced. We may not settle into reception of our breath right off and may need some time to recollect while breathing. And it will include inviting unnecessary concerns to float past, with a promise to return to action on necessary concerns and activities.

As we recollect we may find a peace in our breathing and feel ourselves present to ourselves and in the moment. It is a good natural state of recollection and very good for persons to enter.

Finding the peace given in awareness of the Spirit in our breath is of a higher order than thinking about peace. Using biblical language, we have a fruit of the Holy Spirit in our living relationship, real in every moment and every breath, reaching to me, drawing me in.

And so, breathe attentively and with simple receptivity. Pay attention to your breathing as you settle into your practice. You might consider a pause for receiving your breath now for a moment. When we are new to breathing practice, our goal is attention to our breath. Our minds have a competence at multi-tasking, and so developing the skill of inviting stray thoughts and anxieties to float past us is beneficial.

Breath practice gradually helps to free us from our catalogue of concerns and helps us to be ourselves in the moment. We become aware of our breath and ourselves, prepared and disposed for the deeper awareness of breath, the intimacy of the Spirit, the Breath of God.

Experiencing the Spirit

Even early practice with awareness of the Spirit may be accompanied by what spiritual writers have called a consolation. Our initial breath practice is a meditation and preparation for prayer, prompted by the Spirit who awaits us. The Spirit brings awareness to our minds and the possibility of what Yves Congar would call a touch by the Spirit.

Our practice can lead to a natural, good inner peace, but cannot and does not cause God's action in us. The Spirit awaits us to be open and disposed, giving ourselves over in a certain obedience to the breath given us, learning to breathe in God.

We pray and commune with God in loving response to God's initiative, not for a sensation in prayer. Yet receiving rest in God in time, which of course culminates in eternal communion, is why humanity was created. On the other hand, some spiritual writers, out of concern not to orient persons to some effect of prayer, may practically exclude the joy of God's loving touch or limit it to only a few persons. Doesn't any relationship of love use the energy of the heart and its emotions? Are we conditioned to expect that our relationship with God will be abstract and academic? Our contemporaries, as the earliest Christians, have an instinct that the Spirit intends otherwise.

As the Spirit awaits us, the touch and communion will not appear as coming from outside us, but arising from within, perhaps as a warming consolation of communion, as within is where the Spirit leads us and awaits us.

Awareness of the Word

As we appreciate that God Trinity is not "out there" but facing us, awareness of the Breath of God always present is not a personal aloneness, but leads to a rising awareness of the Word, in whom our lives are inexplicably bound from eternity.

Jesus, the Word Incarnate, becomes fully human so that we enter divinity and Trinitarian communion. It is called *theosis* or divinization. An ancient, ancient maxim of theological faith and Christian anthropology is "God became human so that humans might become God." And Jesus has a human face so that, as God faces humanity directly, we gaze on the very face of God in Jesus and rest in him.

In our practice, we are recollected and disposed to the Spirit bringing awareness of the Spirit's accompaniment of our breath. The Spirit will then dispose us to awareness of Jesus.

The Spirit fosters us to be hearers of Jesus' invitation to communion. I recommend that you not image Jesus in a point of his ministry, or as an infant, or in his passion or resurrection, but rather, as we considered earlier, Jesus the Word in the Prologue of John, and hymns in Ephesians and Colossians. This pancosmic Christ is often found in the icon tradition of the East. These texts can be used in study and reflection so they become our bearing toward the cosmic restoring significance of Jesus and our foreknown presence in Jesus from eternity. The cosmic Christ immersed himself in our humanity and carries it to the Father.

Within our awareness of the Word, I believe the critical awareness of Jesus in our breathing meditation practice was revealed in Scripture where the eternal bridged the temporal, at the Baptism of Jesus, as the voice of the Father identified Jesus as his Beloved. Those words are a conversation within the Trinity. The Father identifies

Jesus as his Beloved. We gaze on and love the Beloved.

Ephesians 1:3–10 takes us further. It is language of intimacy; we are "chosen," "adopted," and "blessed" in Christ, foreknown from all eternity. An astonishing statement follows about the self-gift of God, or grace, that is "bestowed on us in the Beloved."

To me, the Scripture teaches that we are "beloved in the Beloved" with a great significance for the word "in." In Christ, Beloved is our name, too. Your name is Beloved. And so, our awareness is of the breath as well as entering into the Beloved, our true identity, oriented in Christ and through the Spirit to the Father.

Word and Breath are the two Missions of the Father—the two hands of the Father to embrace us and gather us to communion. In receiving the Word and the Breath, we receive Abba, the Father, the Giver who is Gift.

Savor that you are found in the Beloved and that you have this name and identity. Breath brings you to your core; ride your breath. In your core, you find Jesus, who shares his identity of Beloved with you in love. As Beloved we are invited, and in the Beloved we respond.

Gathered in loving communion by the two hands of God, we face the Father, who is source of the circle of love. Some may have a personal history that makes it difficult to pray or rest in the notion of a father. As Beloved in the Beloved, we are given Jesus' own experience of the Father. The two hands of the Father draw us to the Father, who is source, goal, and unity of all. We face God in the Breath and the Beloved.

Henri Nouwen made significant and practical contributions to the theory of ministry and carried the same spirit to his emphasis on our belovedness. He emphasized that it is not an abstraction, but "we must live from it." Simply and powerfully he offers that Beloved "is our primal identity" so that we can flourish and manage our tendencies toward self-rejection, which might be our greatest risk in finding our way to belovedness.

Beloved is our identity and our story. Inspired by Nouwen, I turned to Ephesians as a basis for our location in the Beloved and as Beloved. Further, I believe we can allow our identity as Beloved to grow in our heart and from our heart be expressed in this prayer practice.

You are reading and reflecting on the Beloved Jesus and that we are Beloved in the Beloved. In your prayer practice, breathe awareness of the Spirit and ride your breath to your core, visualized as just below your navel, and as you continue breathing, allow yourself to realize that your breathing has brought you to the Beloved, who shares his name and identity with you, so that you can live in and from it to the Father and to our sisters and brothers. You may have no need for images beyond living awareness of the Breath, the Beloved, and the Father, in whom we live and move and have our being.

Awareness of the Spirit

As we breathe ourselves in the Beloved, we recall the accompaniment of the Spirit, the advocate bestowed by Jesus in Pentecost. Humanity is committed by the Risen Jesus at Pentecost to the Spirit, the Breath, wind, water, and fire of God. The Spirit leads in ways that do not appear linear or predictable, summoning persons who are written off and marginalized.

Spirituality and spiritual practices, I believe, are those means we find to keep us connected to the Spirit of Life. There are many ways of maintaining connection, in reflection, action, personal relationships, presence in our earth, and formal meditation, prayer, and study, including our simple prayer practice that can take us to a deep relationship with God and others. The Spirit prefers the simplest and most common ways to connect. Doesn't breathing seem superbly simple, yet requiring devotion to enter into it?

A prayer to the Holy Spirit in the Eastern Church shows the sweeping presence of the Spirit: "Heavenly king, Consoler, Spirit of Truth, present in all places and filling all things, the treasury of blessings and giver of life, abide in us, cleanse us of all sin, and save our souls, O good one!"

With power that fills all things, the Spirit abides in human persons in a unique manner, drawing inward to communion and energizing us for relationship with God and our sisters and brothers. The Spirit invites all persons to intimate relationship.

Can contemplative practice be expanded for more persons? The Catholic and Orthodox communions, the oldest branches of Christianity, have rightly valued the monastic lives of women and men. Yet as so many writers of the contemplative life have been monastics who taught meditative prayer to other monastics, perhaps countless opportunities to widen meditation practice were lost. In every generation, a range of persons find contemplative living.

Christian history and lives of the saints narrate the contemplative lives of non-monastics. The medieval movement of the Beguines is a clear example of women who lived together, not as vowed religious, yet who left a rich legacy of writings and witness that influenced monastics of their era. It is my hope that persons who might be drawn to prayer of the heart, and are open to the way the Spirit leads us into relationship in the simplicity of breath, will find an invitation to the contemplative way of life in our own everydayness.

Rahner so simply and powerfully said over and over, "Giver and gift are one." God is the self-gift, the self-bestowal. We receive the Giver who is Gift.

God works on and with us from within, helping God's first gift to us, which is our very self, to emerge and be fruitful as life givers ourselves. In our Christian understanding, the theological virtues of faith, hope, and love are works of the Spirit and ourselves. We act more collaboratively than not with the Spirit, to build a relationship for our self-emergence in faith; an orientation to and reliance on the Spirit's nurturance for the now and for future consummation in hope and living in love, the very life and being of God Trinity.

As considered above, the Gifts of the Holy Spirit are given to us for our flourishing, for living from our identity as beloved. The gifts are *wisdom*, which is aligned with love by St. Thomas, *understanding, counsel, knowledge, reverence, fortitude*, and *awe* before God.

In these gifts the Spirit actively illumines, sparks, and fortifies us. Have you noticed awe or wisdom in your life? Have you ever been encouraged to be attentive and aware to identify these good movements as those of the Spirit? St. Thomas takes the gifts very seriously as he takes the active presence of God in us very seriously. Thomas and contemporary theologians such as Karl Rahner, influenced by Thomas and our ancient theological ancestors, find our relationship with God at the heart of being human. Rahner's Christian world is pervaded by the Spirit; we live in a supernatural existential.

Thomas teaches that the Gifts are more important than the theological virtues! He writes that the person is inclined, *inclinatur*, or interiorly moved, *movetur*, to a good state by a gift of the Spirit. A fair translation of *movetur*, in contemporary English, might even be "nudged," alongside "moved" and "touched." Nudging encourages us yet leaves us free to accept or refuse, the cause of much personal and interpersonal suffering.

How does the Spirit act on us? By nudges of love, illumination, insight, reverence, and encouragement. We can be nudged from within, and—just as important—we can be nudged in awareness to have eyes for the work of the Spirit in our brothers and sisters. Awareness of the action of the Spirit in others can be so supportive of our faith in the Spirit's presence and action.

Our work is to give ourselves over to the Spirit as animating force of love. Breathing in God can bring us home to ourselves in the moment and invite the Spirit. And as the gifts are received, so they effect in us the completion of the circle of reception in response.

Effects of the Spirit's action are seen in the fruit of the Spirit, consistent with Jesus' teaching. Yet we can discount or diminish everydayness, looking to dramatic moments. Jesus used the agrarian image of tree-borne fruit, and development in our moral life can be organic, ripening over time. Jesus encourages a good direction that we bear much fruit.

St. Paul finds the human person understandable only in Christ; we live in him and his relationship to the Father in the Spirit. Paul wrote within the early church's experience of the immediate power of the Spirit. In his commentary on Romans, Brendan Byrne considers the Spirit's action as an active inner working, translating Romans 8:15 as "For all whose lives are shaped by the Spirit of God are sons (and daughters) of God."[2]

Participating in the very sonship of Jesus, and Jesus' intimate relationship to the Father, this verse concludes with the sign and expression of this relationship, "We cry out, 'Abba, Father.'"[3] Our prayer of the breath, in which we become aware of the intimate presence of the Breath of God to our breathing, and then awareness of ourselves as Beloved in the Beloved, can turn us in the Beloved to Trinitarian communion in our Abba.

Byrne notes the fascinating significance of "Abba" as the last surviving Aramaic expression in the biblical lexicon as Christians moved into the Greek cultural and intellectual world. "Abba, Father" is Jesus' vocative address to the Father that became that of the earliest Christians, and our own.

Might "Abba" be a most important word for us as Christians? We are face-to-face with our Abba in the face of Jesus and in the Breath received. Abba can become a silent whisper of response with resonance through the cosmos.

Paul contrasts the spirit of slavery to the Spirit of adopted children, and we might ask where it puts us. It seems too easy a question, and we can casually answer that we are children, but we should look further. There might be a middle state in which we know we are God's children but neither have (nor should have) the spirit of slavery and exaggerated fear ... but haven't quite learned to dispose ourselves to the inner Spirit of adoption. That middle state might be one in which one believes in and prays to God and avoids wicked behavior. Here, one can somewhat "manage God" and yet keep God Trinity a bit removed from one's deeper awareness.

Paul coaches us to a deeper and life-giving relationship, which the Spirit is sustaining in all God's children, whether we're aware of it or not. The inner Spirit nudges us to receive God, enter into our identity as Beloved, and respond to God Trinity and to our brothers and sisters. And the inner Spirit prompts us to the confidence of relationship that says with Jesus, "Abba."

Being shaped by the Spirit is ongoing reception for ongoing response. With the gifts of Spirit, we learn to consider awareness, attitudes, and actions before us, and with self-compassion review our awareness, attitudes, and actions. We hold ourselves accountable for them, and turn to the future. Turning to our everydayness, we will develop a loving gratitude for the Spirit's shaping us and the way the gifts inform our loving awareness and loving attitudes for loving action. The gifts, like isotopes, pervade our own lives and that of humanity: "wisdom, understanding, counsel, knowledge, reverence, fortitude and awe."

What does this look like in our everydayness? What do the fruits of the Spirit's working look like? When St. Paul, in Galatians 5:22, identifies the fruits of the Spirit as "love, joy, peace, patience, kindness, goodness, faithfulness, gentleness and self-control," the church is not surprised.[4] With a contemplative gaze, the fruits become apparent, and we see the Breath of God animating them in us and all other persons. It is helpful to memorize the fruits, as they are good to recall, asking to better bear these fruits and to be vigilant to their flourishing in others.

That we bear fruit is our bridge from receiving to responding.

Notes

1. Ruusbroec, "The Spiritual Espousals," in *John Ruusbroec: The Spiritual Espousals and Other Works*, 103. "Ebbing and flowing" is the outgoing-centrifugal and gathering-centripetal love of God in the writings of Blessed John. In his middle Dutch, Abbot Wiseman points out, the word *minne* expressed our common love of God and each other. James A. Wiseman, O.S.B., "*Minne* in *Die Gheestelike Brulocht*," in *Jan van Ruusbroec: The Sources, Content and Sequels of His Mysticism*, eds. F. Mommaers and N. De Paepe (Leuven: Leuven University Press, 1984), 87–99. The article serves as a summary of Abbot James's doctoral dissertation.
2. Brendan Byrne, SJ, *Romans*, 247.
3. Ibid.
4. *Revised Standard Version* (RSV). RSV and the *Revised New Jerusalem Bible* (RNJB) translate *agathosune* as 'goodness.'

CHAPTER 3

Responding

GOD TRINITY IS A sharing life that beckons for response and is always supported synergistically by God; we are not on our own. Centrifugal and centripetal love in creation is God Trinity's invitation for consummation. When we find ourselves within the divine current of love, then response and respond becomes the rhythm of our participation in the divine life and love. Love courses through our being and that of the cosmos.

The goal of this section is one of continued implementation in practice. "Receiving" is the precondition for "responding," the basic theological relational model. A contemporary mind might be tempted to exclude reception in order to "get things going" with "action items" of response.

And so we really can slow down. Receiving is like your in-breath, and response is like your out-breath.

Contemplative living is awareness in this moment, received in what has been called "the interior life," which is not a way to fragment us, but to find the hidden spring of life and love that nourishes and overflows in love.

We have now become aware in practice of our breathing and the intimacy of the Spirit to us, as the Breath of Life. Breath is a powerful, polyvalent word; breath is ours, and it is God's as a tangible presence of the supernatural existential. The Spirit Breath of God accompanies us throughout the course of our days, relationships, and life; our contemplative living is our self-disposal to loving awareness and vigilance, woven into our identity and everydayness.

We will consider three dimensions of responding in love: to God's work in ourselves in self-remembering; to God Trinity; and to our brothers, sisters, and the cosmos.

Responding in Self-Remembering

Christian anthropology lives in understanding the amplitude of what it is to be a person. It gives the basis of the lived Christian life rooted in the foreknowledge of us as Beloved before the cosmos began. We are not an afterthought to God but created as beloved in the Beloved. As Nouwen emphasizes, being beloved is not an abstraction but our primal identity; we are to live from it.

Imagine for a moment another aspect of our identity and an activity flowing from it. It might be caring for a child or another family member, beginning a challenging work project or writing a letter, cooking or gardening. When such work flows from a deep identity within us, it is not simply a task. We find ourselves pulling resources from within, perhaps accompanied by a breath that signals dedication that is under way, so that we can bear down on the work at hand.

Work or relationship flowing from our identity is never an abstraction or thought. Our Christian meditative prayer and contemplative living in God with others can also flow from who we are as beloved. We often need the transition of who we are as beloved to awareness in the moment through self-remembering.

Self-remembering can begin with our breath, aware of breathing first and then of the Spirit who accompanies our breath. Awareness of ourselves as those who breathe with God in the Spirit follows, and then remembering ourselves in the Beloved. We are beloved exactly as who we are, as ourselves now, chosen as Beloved in the Beloved.

As we self-remember, we become aware of the amplitude of being human—that we face God Trinity by our nature. Blessed John Ruusbroec lived and prayed from that truth of inherent relationality. His teaching the inherent "mutual inclination" of God and human persons flows from his confident mystical understanding of relationality.

Self-remembering can correct our orientation and bring us back to a healthy and appreciative self-understanding. We can state, "Yes, in the midst of everything that is pressing on me, I am the beloved." Being beloved is the gift of our identity.

On occasion, awareness may prompt the thought of not living up to my reality in this moment. At other times, we might use a breathing practice to begin a self-review, or examination of conscience. This breathing practice can be an occasion for honesty, insight, renewal, and—most important—confidence in the ongoing restoration wrought by God for living in love. Interestingly, Thich Nhat Hanh teaches that insight about ourselves is a higher goal of meditation, for enlightened expression in compassion.[1]

As we progress in our awareness of the Holy Spirit's presence to us, we should not lose confidence in ourselves regarding everyday lapses. The Greek word *metanoia* means a newness in living and thinking. Perhaps we can remember turns we experienced, similar to the Prodigal Son, who came to himself, in a self-remembering, when he was far from himself, from his identity, and from his Father. We can pray, "Yes, in the midst of my contradictions in living, I am the beloved; help me live consistently, Spirit of God."

Living in the newness of our life in the Beloved Jesus as beloved me, we can have a certain rest and yet always long for greater consistency and flourishing. St. Albert the Great, a medieval Dominican theologian, observer of the natural world, and a teacher of St. Thomas, taught that the spiritual life has an organic growth, not constant progress, with bursts of growth and time to integrate growth. Organic growth means that we are no longer acting out of fear but in response to God's invitation. Like a plant in the garden, we seek light, warmth, and nutrition.

Blessed John Ruusbroec wrote that the person living in relationship with God will experience "daily faults" understood within a perspective of the strength of love. Rather than overemphasizing faults, he brings just the opposite to the person dedicated to the way of growth; "in the loving inward movement" of the person, these daily faults "are just like a drop of water in a red-hot furnace."[2]

A drop of water on a hot pan that we might be preparing for cooking doesn't last long; it disappears. Perhaps a drop of water on a hot pan could be a spiritual exercise for giving God's love our everyday shortcomings. Faith and hope in God's loving renewal can also prompt an honest review of shortcomings in attitudes and actions. What a confident statement from our spiritual master Blessed John, and so much in contrast from those who only see faults and would obsess about others with every minor failing, sometimes taking away their hope for a vibrant relationship with God. Our core identity is not sinner but beloved.

Self-remembering supports who we are. It is a process of recollecting the astonishing identity we bear as beloved in the Beloved. Remembering who we are orients us to respond to God Trinity and to our brothers, sisters, and the cosmos. Remembering carries contentment, gratitude, praise, and a smile that surfaces to show the integration of our being.

Responding to God in Group or Liturgical Prayer

Responding occurs as the person we are in the moment and as we emerge over the moments and years. We might have begun our experience of prayer with reciting prayers, and as a child, it could carry important family, church, community, or cultural notes. Religion is necessarily interpersonal; the culture of community can be foundational.

Spoken prayer that we compose or share within the church community is as old a practice as God's call to Abraham, our father in faith. It is a manifestation of our communal reception of and response to divine life given us. The Eastern and Western branches of Christianity gather on Sunday for the divine liturgy, to celebrate the Lord's resurrection, renewal of humanity in his own life, and orientation to the consummation of history in Trinitarian communion.

On a daily basis, the sister churches of East and West celebrate the sacredness of time in the divine office or liturgy of the hours, with psalms, Scripture readings, writings of ancient Christian ancestors, and prayers over the course of the day. And the year is marked by the liturgical cycle of celebrations in the pattern of salvation history, as we look forward to history's consummation, the point omega of the fullness of God's reign and plan of love.

Our breathing meditation practice of reception and self-remembering doesn't have to be separate from the response of formal prayer. Meditation itself doesn't have to be formal or lengthy. In life we are given moments. Unique settings and occasions can recall us to ourselves in any moment, as we begin personal prayer or study and in the midst of communal or liturgical prayer. We can return to ourselves and invoke the Spirit as we prepare to read Scripture or hear it liturgically proclaimed. It can help us bring ourselves to this prayer, placing us in the moment, and putting aside that which should be set aside for this prayer, and animating rituals so that the actions are not ends in themselves.

Breathing practice brings us to a moment of responding. First, bring attention to your breath, and then invite awareness of the Spirit accompanying your breathing, and awareness of being the beloved who you are.

If you are open to an imageless way to the Father in communion with the Son and Spirit Breath, we learn from Blessed John, a great teacher of imageless contemplation, a blossoming of prayer using images toward the mutual inclination of God and the person.

The moment of receiving the breath can bring us to spoken or liturgical prayer, or to breathe ourselves into a simple prayer of thanksgiving before a cup of tea or a meal, in which we can be more attentive to the persons with whom we are gathered and to the fruit of the earth before us, that can be received with simple joy and gratitude. Breath practice brings us to the moment we have, to enter into it with a greater and growing awareness and appreciation.

Liturgical prayer merits attention as work of the community. When we use breath practice to enter into it, we can bring awareness of ourselves in the moment as well as our brothers and sisters around the world, and those who have gone before us, singing to God Trinity.

A particular example of liturgical life is participating in the Eucharist and the reception of Jesus in communion. The most ancient traditions in the Eastern and Western Churches continuously hold that in the invocation of the Holy Spirit, *epiclesis*, the species of bread and wine on the altar, are fundamentally transformed to the presence of Jesus for us, as a foretaste of the eternal feast of the New Jerusalem when this age is consummated in glory.

Breath practice can be used in holy communion to deepen our experience of this moment. We can breathe our way in walking to communion, in the very reception, in the walk to our place and the moments of presence to the eucharist received, and to our gathered community of love.

Recall how we follow our breath inward, to the core of our being. Imagine our breathing practice following communion. We receive the Breath of God in our breath, and in this moment we receive Jesus, the Word of God in the eucharistic species. Both missions of God, Word and Breath, have actually entered us and are coursing through us! The missions travel within us, to bring us within ourselves to God's dwelling, as a source of reverence and joy beyond telling.

Those of us who received communion even as children might remember that the inwardness of communion, the very gift of Godself, had carried us inward. Communion is perhaps the most gripping example of the sensuality of Christianity, a literal physical oneness with God that, were it not given by Jesus himself at the Last Supper, would have been too extreme for a human to propose. Hence the significance of eucharistic spirituality in the churches over the centuries.

Medieval churches used the colors of the natural world, green for vegetation and blue for the sky, with columns standing in for trees, to evoke a world inside the church building. It wasn't to take worshippers out of this world in an abstract way, but to invite them into a new way of living here. The earth colors stand for a paradise of relationships regained when Christians give themselves over to the Holy Spirit, who develops us into the person God knows us to be. The church is the place where the faithful are pervaded by the bread the Holy Spirit has taken for a new purpose, and we, too, can be transformed to live in a paradisical life in a continuing way. Such is the power of the liturgical experience and imaginary.

A significant devotional exercise is eucharistic devotion in the Western Church. It differs a bit from the typical visit to church for fruitful prayer, as we saw in Dorothy Day's New York City parish. In the traditional visit, the Eucharist, or Blessed Sacrament, would be quietly reserved within the tabernacle, and individuals could pray as they wish there, often in response to the eucharistic presence of Jesus. In eucharistic adoration, a single larger host is placed for greater visibility and prayer response in a *monstrance*, from the Latin word to show or make visible.

In eucharistic presence in the simple visit, as well as in times of eucharistic adoration, persons may briefly visit or commit to a longer period. We can run the risk in adoration of becoming abstract or solely doctrinal; an affirmation of faith in the presence of Jesus can become a "you are there." At times of faith development, a doctrinal focus might have a beneficial dimension, but could become an extrinsic experience. Using breathing practice in adoration, we receive the breath and the Spirit who accompanies our breathing. Then, in the spirit of reception, we are disposed to receive the power and presence of Jesus, who is admittedly a bit distant from us, but not at all limited by it.

In this moment, he can become not out-there but here-for-us, his loving power streaming to us with our in-breath and our love returning with our out-breath. No images are needed. This is prayer of the heart. It is the simple received mysticism of countless Christians who have gone before us.

The two missions or two hands of God are present to us for our response, to God Trinity and overflowing to those gathered with us and to all persons in love.

The eucharistic sensuality of Christianity can be a perfect opportunity for bringing together our intellectual dimension and heart. If our challenge is to bridge the distance between mind and heart, breath meditation can support the integration. The meditation takes our intellectual moment of awareness within us, not to analyze the mystery of the presence of Jesus to and for us, but to welcome it as we ride the awareness inward with our breath to communion.

Growth or Stages in the Spiritual Life

Over the centuries, Christian writers who have written on inner animation, or spiritual life, recognized its developmental nature. A healthy attitude is one of a positive sense of growth. The frightful opposite is *acedia* or sloth, the last of the seven vices, a turning away from and boredom with even considering the inner font of life.

We shouldn't try to quantify levels or stages as much as recognize patterns of response or non-response to God. This is our theme of "responding," and where we see responding, we find the prompting of the Holy Spirit.

Blessed John represents the older European contemplative tradition; I find connection with those who lived in fidelity to the Spirit and taught the way to be nurturing. John calls for a conversion of heart as an ongoing turning to God and a turning from or dying to inauthentic or other destructive living. Our spiritual desire for life in the Trinity of love nudges us to ever more authentic living.

He writes that spiritual or inner animated living is not our doing alone, as we are always responding, or not, to God. God invites with a grace that is "prevenient" or beckoning us to accept.[3] Growth in the virtues follows love, which is the "fountainhead of all virtue."[4]

In his *Little Book of Clarification*, which is a lovely later summary writing, Blessed John teaches that all persons are called to a living union with God. He proposes two ways: union with intermediaries and union without intermediaries, the imageless way. Blessed John teaches that we all rely on intermediaries, the chief of which are the two missions of God for us. As Christianity is an incarnational and sensual religion, our relationship within God is expressed and supported by thoughts, words, songs and chant, images and icons, light and darkness, smells, tastes, processions, and a range of physical postures.

Prayer and union with intermediaries can be furthered by our breathing practice of love to a greater awareness and participation; it is a vibrant contemplative way, and the typical spiritual practice in the Eastern and Western Churches. In Blessed John's teaching, encouraged in our practice, prayer and union without intermediaries lives with and is nourished by them, and in a way uses them to encounter God in an imageless way. It is a path less taken.

I believe that as we deepen our breathing-based Trinitarian contemplative way, riding the breath inward, we can find a pathway both to love the images and go beyond them in encounter.

Traditional discursive meditation that grew within the *lectio divina* tradition is prayer with intermediaries, yet one that desires to be carried beyond itself in love by the Holy Spirit. Franciscan Richard Rohr shared his experience with discursive meditation, and the barrier of seeming a practice of meditative *thinking* to many. "They still called it mental prayer when I was a novice in 1961, but it was largely about concentrating, which, of course, does not work. Most gave up on prayer very early—without realizing that they had."[5]

Centering prayer is based on a personally chosen word or phrase for meditative repetition; some incorporate attention to breath for recollection. It intends to be "wholly present" and utterly open to God for progression to silence.[6] It has proven itself as a foundational form of discursive meditation for countless persons.

Our breathing in God practice finds a necessary place for study and prayer with ideas and words, and it transitions to another path of moments of awareness. Our breath offers an occasion to remember who we are in the Breath and the Beloved; that God Trinity, in centripetal love, draws us inward to communion beyond thoughts and words.

Sacraments and sacramentals are encounters with God and intermediaries of which Blessed John writes; they are hallowed by the devotion of our ancestors over the millennia, centuries, and today. Words are ours for self-expression and communion, and so words are natural for prayer.

Prayer with intermediaries requires the spirit of devotion, that is, lifting up the mind and heart (a classical understanding) to God as awareness in love. We can be troubled or distracted, without the focus we want, yet God is constantly present within and for us in our moment. This type of prayer is oriented to God, of course, and in the fullness of response, can carry us to our sisters and brothers.

What of the times when we feel we can't pray? Henri Nouwen guides us and provides reassurance that "our emotional life is not the same as our spiritual life." Our emotions rise and fall; he reminds us to reconnect with our primal identity as God's children.

Spiritual life is animation by the Spirit within. Blessed John teaches that our spiritual life, as we deepen it, becomes a flowing of love back and forth, with what he rightly calls a mutual delight and contentment in God Trinity and human persons. Our starting point tends to be external movement from ourselves to God. In meditation we can shift toward an inward movement to God within and God's movement to us from within.

Blessed John knows human reasoning and our need to turn inward to meet God. "Christ comes to us from within outward, while we come to him from without inward."[7] Breathing practice brings us inward and, as we noted earlier, can be both a fine preparation for prayer with intermediaries and imageless prayer without intermediaries.

Jewish and Christian Scriptures, as well as Christian writers over the centuries, were more aware of the gift of breath than ourselves. Ours now is the opportunity to recover this awareness for practice in any setting, any moment across the span of our life.

As we devote time to learning to breathe and then grow through enlightened loving awareness of the Spirit, we can recover ourselves for disposition for vocal prayer, liturgy, or meditative reading and the lived moments of everydayness. Our moments become more unified.

We become more able to turn inward to communion or rest in God. Breathing practice brings us back to ourselves so that we can be aware of God who faces us, not as a question to be solved, but in the darkness of inner love. Our practice can dispose us for the spirit of recollection, integrating mind and heart in love for prayer with intermediaries. It can dispose us to take the next step of imageless contemplative prayer, prayer without intermediaries, according to the teaching and tradition of Ruusbroec.

Blessed John recognizes that a small number of persons will experience prayer without intermediaries. A contributing reason is that it had not been widely experienced or taught; he devoted himself to this teaching, however, and it is critical to sustain and expand access to our form of prayer.

There is fulfillment and good life in his "prayer with intermediaries," as it is common to us all and our shared path of life in the Spirit. At different stages of life, we will find or rediscover spiritual practices. "Prayer without intermediaries" and then "prayer without difference" in lived oneness with God Trinity are both grounded in the Christian life; they can arise when a person is guided into an obedience to the Spirit in quiet prayer, or prayer of the heart. Our breathing practice follows Blessed John for your invitation to the quiet reception of the Spirit inward without images.

Our Lived Practice

The Spirit guides us to practice in contemplative living.

First, we accept our breath to return to ourselves in self-remembering. At times, one or two breaths might bring us home; more settling might be needed in the course of the day.

Second, we receive awareness of the Spirit breathing the primordial gift of breath to humanity. We may be invited to dwell and rest in the Breath of God and rest in the Spirit Breath of love. Awareness is not a reflection on a text we read, but a simple loving awareness.

Third, we receive awareness of Jesus the Beloved, in a loving reception of the Beloved in which we may be invited to dwell and abide in him. The Spirit brings us to the Beloved, aware that we are Beloved in the Beloved prior to the birth of the cosmos. Again, it is not discursive reflection on Scripture; we have done that work already and will return to Scripture again and again for deeper nourishment and knowledge. Now, we can sigh a simple loving awareness of and longing for the Beloved—not thinking about it but receiving it in awareness, without images, without intermediaries, as Blessed John wrote.

Fourth, we come to awareness that we are enfolded in the Word and the Breath of God, the missions, the hands and arms of Abba Father, and in this embrace are brought to the Father in Trinitarian communion.

Throughout his writings, Blessed John teaches that we can be brought, over time and through our faithful reception and response, to an imageless state. A certain bareness of thought, or beyondness of thought, to an imageless state of communion. It is a rest, yet not always a quiet rest, of the drawing inward to ourselves where God Trinity meets us in mutual contentedness.

In our personal ways of prayer life, we may have received particular moments of clarity or peace or unbounded love in God that embraces. Looking back, we may have had these moments even in our childhood; such is the Spirit's work of mystical or enlightening gifts across the life-span.

Over the years, we can experience both growth and setbacks in our life in God, yet the Spirit beckons. We might remember an earlier insight that can renew us.

Yves Congar, the great theologian of the Word and the Breath, suggests that we can intentionally "give ourselves over to the Spirit" in our relations with God and our brothers and sisters. And we should do so by intentional practice, I believe, because the Spirit was given to us without reservation at Pentecost. If the Spirit is given us, should we not give ourselves over in response, like the mutuality within the Trinity?

Congar also suggests the simple, ancient, and beautiful prayer, "Come Holy Spirit, fill the hearts of your faithful," as a way of turning ourselves to the Spirit in this moment. Contemporary theologian Leonardo Boff finds the ancient hymn *Veni, Creator Spiritus,* "Come, Holy Spirit, Creator blest" particularly significant:

> This is perhaps the most important prayer that believers can raise to the Holy Spirit. The Spirit is the wind from God that swept over the face of the waters in creation (Genesis 1:1–2), coming and going over the primitive chaos (alternative potentialities), bringing the universe and all beings into existence. In trinitarian terms, the three divine Persons always act together. They all participate in the creative act.... We invite the Creator Spirit to visit our souls and fill our hearts with its grace. Indeed, the Spirit is the sacred flame burning within us.... We pray that its creative activity will infuse our life projects.[8]

We invoke the Spirit who rejoices to dwell within, as Blessed John teaches that God comes to us not from outside but from within. When we pray "Come Holy Spirit" over the course of our day and years, it is to dispose us for the Spirit's emergence within our hearts, for personal guidance and response.

Christian breathing practice invokes the Spirit of love, who is given us as guide and companion; it is explicitly Trinitarian, as the missions of the Word and Spirit Breath are for communion with the Beloved's Abba. We dispose ourselves to the inward and imageless pathway and are taken into the circle of love that has its own course.

Our guide in all forms of prayer and in all aspects of life is the Spirit. Blessed John's teaching on prayer has been most beneficial in developing our way of prayer. The Spirit of love will guide each of us in our own relationship and experience, using teachers like Blessed John who have been given to us over the centuries.

We should progress and yet be patient with ourselves. An observation of St. Thomas seems fitting: "that which is received is received according to the mode of the receiver" or *quidquid recipitur recipitur secundum modum recipientis*. While often used in philosophical discussions, Congar rightly applies the insight to our life in the Spirit. We might need support in remembering that God is given to us as Beloved, and we in our very core are Beloved, or that all others, too, are Beloved in the Beloved. The Spirit cares for us as known and loved unique persons, at our stage of life, in our moment.

We can follow the Spirit for loving response in prayer with intermediaries. We can also follow the Spirit in loving reception and response through the intermediaries to imageless loving communion. Blessed John teaches that the path of resting in God[9] is an active emptiness[10] and a gaze.[11]

Trinitarian breathing prayer has helped me bring Blessed John's teaching into practice. The Spirit gives for our own personal reception, *secundum modum recipientis*, so that there can be as many accounts of experience of the Spirit as there are those who can receive the movement and initiative of the Spirit. Our own life in the Spirit will not be like a textbook; it is unique to ourselves.

Receiving our breath is a recovery of the ancient Jewish and Christian incarnational spirituality for our integrated spirituality. Again, in its full form, breathing intentionally and with awareness is a first step in practice, followed by receiving awareness of the Spirit whose presence accompanies our prayer; followed by receiving awareness of the Beloved and our Belovedness, all toward the Father as both source, goal, and bond of communion in the Word and in the Breath. With each step of awareness, we can further give ourselves over to the dynamic of love that draws us into love, like a stream that can be a peaceful flow, or breaks out into a faster pace.

There will be times when our practice might be a brief self-recovery. Throughout the day we might begin, *first*, with just an intentional breath or two, in which our awareness is of our breath, and *second*, receive a living awareness of the Spirit, the Breath within the breath. As we ride our breath, the Spirit's inner presence emerges for our accompaniment. It is the gift of communion, familiarity, and relatedness; love. Self-recovery may develop into a most abiding dimension of your contemplative practice, as simple response in relationship to God.

Writing in Japan in the 1970s, William Johnston noted that "It is a wonderful fact of experience that, in those who have faith, mindfulness of the breathing can lead to a relishing of the presence of the Spirit. Some people's meditation consists in just breathing silently and wordlessly in the Spirit."[12]

Responding to God happens in unique moments of prayer and action. Response to God is led by the Spirit, and it is not complete without responding to our brothers and sisters and caring for creation in a new relationship of responsibility.

Responding to Others

Christianity is about the good news of our relatedness to God Trinity and each other. Christianity is not primarily a school of ethics, yet it needs ethical practice to live its proclamation of unity. Response to others is our starting and ending point. If Christianity is our life in God Trinity and divinization as the Beloved, then our care for our Beloved sisters and brothers can become more vibrant, animated by the Spirit.

Our Jewish and Christian traditions and experiences are explicitly relational. God forms a people in relationship with God and each other.

Over the course of our life, there are times we need norms in our relations with others; they represent the experience of the community and its openness to ongoing learning. Beyond and more energetic than norms are the positive dynamics within our lives in human community and culture, or in sub-culture experiences. Professions such as teaching, agriculture, nursing, medicine, and ministry can be seen as subcultures with their own historical self-understanding that can nourish individuals and provide an experience of collegiality for the group. Compassion and competence might be fundamental elements in the *ethos* of the professions.

Response to God and one another is the leitmotif used by Bernard Häring in his second masterwork of moral theology, *Free and Faithful in Christ*. Conscience is often the responsibility we have as individuals, yet relationship is the context of humanity. Persons are called to communal recognition in a "reciprocity of consciences," as understanding has an inherently social dimension. Häring identifies the fullness of "conscience" as a knowing-with others.[13]

The teachings of Jesus nudge us to the dynamic of loving response to persons. His words often pointed to the heart as the inner core of persons, the source of attitudes and actions that are praiseworthy or to be condemned. In the Last Supper discourse of John 15, Jesus appeals to his disciples gathered around him to abide in him and become the heart of our response to persons. In the course of verses 4–10, the word abide/remain appears ten times! What could be a more emphatic invitation to the inwardness of God for us? God's work is on our heart as the source of renewed attitudes and action.

From the heart comes response—hence, Niebuhr's and Häring's emphasis on response that renewed contemporary moral theology. When we respond from the heart stirred in breath awareness, the truth of our identity emerges for the other person.

Our responding comes from the heart and who we are; our primal identity is Beloved. Beloved is expressed in you so that you can encounter the other as one Beloved to another Beloved.

When considering the Beloved in Scripture, we have used two citations so far. The first is the Baptism of Jesus, in which the Trinity is revealed and we hear the inner conversation of the Trinity, naming Jesus as the Beloved. The second is from the Letter to the Ephesians, in which we hear ourselves as Beloved in the Beloved. And now a third, in St. Paul's Letter to the Colossians (3:12–17), in which we are called as chosen and beloved, to teach us as Beloved how to live:

> As God's chosen ones, holy and beloved, clothe yourselves with compassion, kindness, humility, meekness, and patience.... Above all, clothe yourselves with love, which binds everything together in perfect harmony.... And whatever you do, in word or in deed, do everything in the name of the Lord Jesus, giving thanks to God the Father through him.

Three truths unfold in these Scriptures: Jesus is the Beloved; we are Beloved in the Beloved; and we are to act as Beloved to our Beloved sisters and brothers, in the Belovedness of Jesus the eternal Son of God. We can begin with the inbreathing of receptivity as Beloved to respond with the outgoing breath of love.

Acting as Beloved can be a good way to call ourselves to awareness, attitude, and actions. We might often have heard in homilies or read in spiritual texts that we should imitate Christ in our actions. That might be a bit off-putting, as Jesus lived in a particular culture and period of time. We might naturally find it difficult to transpose ourselves to Jesus and his context; can we go beyond this barrier?

Yet St. Paul reminds us that living "in" Christ is our truth; that we are Beloved in the Beloved. And so, we are not called to imitate his actions exactly as the Spirit moved him. Rather, we as Beloved are called to find ourselves in the pancosmic heart of Jesus and to live as the Beloved we find ourselves to be. Living in the Beloved Jesus helps our truth to emerge over time.

Being in Christ and in the Spirit facilitates our response as acting persons equipped in the Spirit's gifts of wisdom, counsel, understanding, knowledge, reverence, courage, and awe (based on Isaiah 11:2). We live in the theological virtues of faith, hope, and love. Faith brings us into reliance on the energy of God for us, to live in and as the Beloved. And sustained by the Spirit, we bear fruit of love, joy, peace, patience, kindness, goodness, faithfulness, gentleness, and self-control (Galatians 5:22). There are countless expressions of Christian living, but the foundation of gifts, theological virtues, and fruit are what our tradition sees as the trajectory of living in truth as the Beloved.[14]

Our responding is the everydayness of life in Christ and the Spirit. Receiving the incoming breath can position us for response in the breath of love. In our daily responsibilities we are caught up in the flow of many demands and activities; they are our path of ongoing response. Thus, we must not feel guilty for not having awareness of the gift of the breath and the presence of the Spirit at every moment. Such is our graced life now. When we intentionally accept our breath at moments of quiet awareness, we may find in demands of challenge that we can be renewed and brought back.

Over time, the Spirit will continue to shape us as persons of receptivity and response to deepen our moments in the flow of activity. We Christians hold action and response as an essential mark of our fidelity to our identity and to God's way and reign in history. But we should not separate it from receptivity to God as if our response were simply our own capacity. Response is like the beautiful out-breath; it cannot last and needs the next given in-breath!

We receive love to respond in love, and drawing close to the Spirit in love will prompt love, for as Blessed John taught, love is "the beginning and fountainhead of all virtues."[15] Love is interwoven by God in us and directed to God and to others who are in God as well. Come Holy Spirit, come from within me to awaken me and sustain me in loving response. Come Holy Spirit.

Everydayness of love is our world. The uniqueness of persons summons us to response. If our everydayness has the good fortune of relative calm and order, we should learn to rely on the Spirit for ongoing openness, encounter, and responsiveness to persons.

The everydayness of breathing and receiving continues to dispose us to the Spirit's action and gifts that bear fruits of love, joy, peace, patience, kindness, goodness, faithfulness, gentleness, and self-control. The fruits of the Spirit come forth in our everydayness, the soil in which we are planted.

The gifts and fruits are so intended for intentional and peaceful, moment-to-moment living. We might also recall that the fruits of the earth burst forth for a moment of ripeness. The Spirit waters, prunes, and brings forth our fruitfulness.

Contemplative living brings pained awareness that countless persons do not enjoy even a relative calm. Matthew 25 reminds us that Jesus self-identifies with marginalized and overlooked persons, as well as individuals who experience sudden or lifelong distress or persecution.

Leonardo Boff writes of the ways the Spirit rouses us to response. The contemplative person can launch into action, moved by the Spirit:

> The hymn ends by asking the Spirit to keep us always open and alert to "what God wants us to hear." The Spirit does not speak directly into our ears. It awakens us to the signs of the times, the urgent needs of others, the situation of the world, the miserable fate of the poor. God is always sending us messages. The Spirit keeps us on alert, because each time it comes is a unique moment. As one of the pre-Socratic philosophers said: "If we don't expect the unexpected, when it happens we will not see it." The Spirit is like that. It is a gentle breeze, not a whirlwind. It is a whisper, not a yell. To hear and understand it we have to be mindful, with open and attentive hearts.[16]

Boff relies on the attentive heart for understanding and action. The contemplative activist experiences God's sustenance; recall Dorothy Day at prayer in the parish church in lower Manhattan. Her activism was sustained by her contemplative spirit. Thomas Merton taught the essential need of contemplation for meaningful action. St. Francis of Assisi devoted himself to reconciliation that arose from his contemplative experience. We are invited to weave the two together as one in our life. The weaving can begin as we receive the breath and the Spirit, for response.

Sometimes in our breath practice we experience distractions. These should be sorted out. A thought about an enjoyable food is good but might be a genuine distraction in prayer; encourage it to drift by as if on the breeze. However, a thought about a meal that I will prepare for the family or a form of assistance I will perform for a person in need is not a classic distraction. It is a thought of love for love.

The act of love is a response to others as my prayer is a response to God, which also prepares me in the circle of love to respond to others in love. Perhaps we can thank the thought for being a response to others and reminding us to integrate our action with love. But we might then ask the thought of doing good to return a little later as we follow our breath and self-remembering to our core, which also prepares us for action.

The direction our prayer will take will vary day by day. At times we will follow the thought about making a meal for those we love because it might be time to begin the meal preparation; this is responding to God and others in the moment. At other times we should follow the breath inward in awareness of ourselves, the Spirit, the Word, and the Father. Our prayer will bear the fruit of an overflowing love that will prepare us to work on the meal.

Classical Christian humanism is attentive to the earth and its peoples. It is intentional in planning for the common good and meaningful inclusion of marginalized and oppressed persons. Rejoice in actions for the good of the Mother Earth and her peoples!

St. Thomas Aquinas' writings long ago challenged me in a simple and elegant statement about peace as relational, and the either/or of choosing self alone or inclusion of others in justice. "Peace breaks down when individual citizens seek only their own interests."[17] For Thomas and ancient Christian social theology, peace is not the absence of hostility. Injustice can happen very quietly and methodically. Peace is an order of right relationships; it breaks down when we seek solely our own interests or the interests of a group to further fragment humanity.

We can increasingly live from our primal reality as Beloved. Living from our reality, to me, means reliance on the Word and the Breath, the two hands, the two missions of God, for the deep passion of contemplative action.

Notes

1 Thich Nhat Hanh, *How to Sit*, 78.

2 Ruusbroec, "The Spiritual Espousals," 136.

3 Ibid., 44.

4 Ibid., 49.

5 Richard Rohr, *Silent Compassion: Finding God in Contemplation* (Cincinnati, OH: Franciscan Media, 2014), 70.

6   John Main, *Fully Present: The Daily Path of Christian Meditation*, ed. Laurence Freeman (Maryknoll, NY: Orbis Books, 2014), 30.

7   Ruusbroec, "Spiritual Espousals," 117.

8   Leonardo Boff, *Come, Holy Spirit: Inner Fire, Giver of Life, and Comforter of the Poor*, trans. Margaret Wilde (Maryknoll, NY: Orbis Books, 2015), 191. His reflection is within a larger meditation on hymns to the Spirit, 183–198.

9   Ruusbroec, "Spiritual Espousals," 67, 70, 95, 99, 108, 136.

10   Ibid., 136.

11   Ibid., 244–245.

12   William Johnston, "The Inner Eye of Love," in *Lord Teach Us to Pray*, 354.

13   Häring, *Free and Faithful*, 265–267.

14   Leonardo Boff is an example of a contemporary theologian who gives particular attention to the dynamic significance of the gifts and fruits of the Spirit; see *Come, Holy Spirit*, 175–179.

15   Ruusbroec, "Spiritual Espousals," 49. St. Thomas teaches love as the source and form of the virtues.

16   Leonardo Boff, *Come Holy Spirit*, 198. Boff's earlier *Holy Trinity, Perfect Community* (Maryknoll, NY: Orbis Books, 2000) is a Trinitarian theology that explicates the doctrine and puts it into practice as our liberation program as persons invited into communion with God and humanity. In his essential *Toward an Eco-Spirituality* (New York: Crossroad, 2015), Boff presents the weave of spiritual commitment to the Earth as the basis for action in the essential and undeniable imperative to respond to Mother Earth.

17   *Summa Theologiae* II-II, 183, 2 ad 3; my translation.

PART III

Living with Ourselves and Others

Living in a dynamic urban culture, second-century Christian philosopher and theologian Clement of Alexandria addressed a wide range of persons who were becoming Christians. He used the literature of his era as both pointing to the Christian understanding of the human person and to divergences. Clement taught Christ as the teacher of humanity, and humanity as God's project, humanity as God's work of art: "Who breathed life into man? Who gave him the sense of right? Who has promised immortality? None but the Creator of the universe, the 'Father, the supreme artist,' formed such as living statue as man...."[1]

Clement's was a beautiful and stirring vision; our earliest Christian ancestors held humanity in such high regard! That we are God's works of art might be why we find each other fascinating and attractive, and with a common bond as brothers and sisters beloved of God.

Ancient Christians entered into the Scripture's vision of humanity as foreknown and loved from eternity in the Beloved. Growth in the fullness of our humanity is growth in the gift of participation in divinity by divinization, or *theosis*. In recent centuries, with the rise of empiricism, Christians have lost their grasp on the glory of their humanity as fundamentally related to God and to each other.

We, on the other hand, live in an era in which our self-description of ourselves tends to be a bio-chemical, consumerist, and individualist reductionism. Jesus slips away as our model of Beloved and leader in time and eternity. At times, however, the dynamic vision of Scripture and our ancient Christian ancestors breaks through.

It can be challenging to hold humanity and ourselves in high regard, as we live in a broken world and can be quite broken ourselves. St. Paul writes that the world is "yearning for healing and completion." We believe that healing transformation is under way, but if our modern understanding of God puts God at a distance, we can quite naturally lose faith in ourselves along the way.

When God is extrinsic, which is the common contemporary sense, we can feel ourselves to be worlds distant from God and far from faith's life-giving relational immediacy. The ancients and our prayer practice invite an alternative in a shift to the interior activity of God. It all began with the breath, God's intimate presence to the soil and dust animated as Adam.

The creation account of Genesis 2:7 conveys God's intimacy to the carbon dust of the cosmos by God's own animating breath. Prayer experience of breathing in God recalls and renews our creation intimacy in us.

American Lutheran theologian Joseph Sittler commented prior to a 1959 lecture that Genesis "is not zoology but the disclosure of the amplitude of human life, the breath of God." Our breathing-in-God prayer practice recovers the power of breath in Scripture and our tradition for our moment. Are we up for the amplitude of our human life? The Spirit accompanies us in patient urging and does not leave us alone.

Reception-response is the cycle of inner Trinitarian life. It is extended to us in each breath as invitation to awareness or enlightenment. We are made for the now, and breathing takes us there in the Spirit, as ourselves.

Becoming and Being Ourselves

God Trinity's ongoing active intimacy recalls us to our dignity and God's presence in the gift of wisdom. A fruit of the Spirit is patience, even with ourselves. Breathing in God, relying on the presence of the Spirit, can help our self-critique and our self-acceptance and self-patience.

Patience permits development of the virtues or strengths of Christian life, identified as theological faith, hope, and love, as well as the classical philosophical virtues of humanity, prudence (appreciating the "big picture" of life, decisions, and outcomes), justice, temperance (or restraint and self-control), and courage. They will, in our synergy with the Holy Spirit, organically grow with attention and self-criticism, as well as self-compassion.

Karl Rahner encouraged a reflective meditation on our baptism for renewal:

> Yet in daily life we might also once in a while tell ourselves explicitly, "You have been baptized. The Holy Spirit lives and wants to operate at the innermost core of your being. God has called you by your name, sanctifying and divinizing you. God wishes this divine life to grow strong in your life, all the way down to the smallest details. It is not enough for you to be sealed with the Holy Spirit, you must also bring forth the fruits of the Spirit, which according to Paul are love, joy, peace, patience, goodness, fidelity, meekness and self-control." When we try in this way explicitly to remember our baptismal grace and expressly urge ourselves to live out of its spirit and power, we explicitly renew our baptism. If we seriously mean it and honestly try to do what we prompt ourselves to do, baptismal grace really increases, it acquires increasing influence in our life, and we become what we were in the seed planted at baptism: Christians.[2]

As we rely on the Holy Spirit as our inner power and teacher, enlightening our vision and way, we can become friends of time for our own development. Our selves emerge over time in God's wraparound, patient love. Might we regularly pause for a spiritual review to appreciate our emerging selves and our actualization as Beloved in the Beloved?

Our experience of the demands and concerns of moment count. At times we struggle with even a simple spoken prayer. Breathing practice is not only for times of quiet! We might simply catch our breath in the moment to help stabilize us in the midst of flux. A moment or two later, on another breath, we might self-remember or be aware of the presence of the Spirit within, ever so briefly, but for a consolation and encouragement for our persistence.

We have previously noted that we find ourselves so much in the flow of a creative or committed action that we might even lose a sense of our body; we become one with the activity. A good and compassionate committed action, such as care for a spouse, child, or elder, must summon our full attention. Our intention is to be in accord with God's way, and we can breathe ourselves into committed activity over the course of the day.

Ancient Christians prayed the Lord's Prayer three times a day as a commitment to God's Kingdom or reign, which was a prime focus of Jesus' preaching. Jesus is the visible presence of the Father's reign, and we pray commitment to it by entering into Jesus and his commitment. The prayer calls for God's will of loving and just commitment to be manifest in the halting steps of our day. And the prayer expresses our reliance on our loving Abba, in Jesus.

We can pray this, which Jesus gave us in a renewed recollection, by breathing our way into it. It is the Spirit Breath of God who calls out Abba Father within us, as St. Paul writes. Blessed John wrote that "Abba is a song that the Father loves us to sing." Abba can take us into the Lord's Prayer, summoned by the breath of God in love, for love.

Prayer to God-Abba, as we suggested, is renewed when we find ourselves and our identity in Jesus the Beloved. We enter into Jesus' own experience and relationship to his Abba. Rowan Williams wrote that "It seems that all Christian reflection, all theology worth the name, began as people realized that because of Jesus Christ they could talk to God in a different way.... The new way we talk to God is as Father, and that is the work of the Spirit of Jesus.... And the prayer that Jesus himself taught his disciples expresses this very clearly: 'Our Father.'"[3]

We might ask ourselves if we are ready to go beyond the thought of being Beloved to actually becoming the Beloved. Our breathing practice invites us to take that step toward enlightened awareness. It should be preceded by study and reflection of the love between Jesus and his Abba, and on Jesus' commitment to the way or reign (*basileia*) of his Father, so that it becomes our way in both the most momentous and the smallest responses and actions. Aristotle observed in *Nicomachean Ethics* that the way to be just is to repeatedly act justly; human growth is organic. All will increasingly flow from our emerging and ratified identity as beloved.

Contemplative Everydayness

Growing in identity with Jesus the Beloved, our everydayness can become contemplative living. Contemplation is the gift of awareness of relationship in the Holy Spirit. We come to ourselves through breathing in God and then acting from the truth of who we are.

Renewal in the moment brings our truth to working or walking, cooking, eating, or washing up. Experiencing a gentle breeze or strong wind can become new and deeply meaningful when it becomes a symbol of God's cosmic and intimate Breath. We receive it as well as feel it.

In breathing practice, the moment can become one of contemplative relational awareness and reception that is appreciative and active. As we enter into our life activities, we will often pour ourselves into it, which is just fine.

Creative activity doesn't deplete us; immersing in commitment is part of the creativity. Perhaps during or as we complete a committed work we remember Love again. Love emerges for the moment. Breathing brings us to ourselves as beloved, and breathing practice takes us to everything, held together by the active love of God in the world.

As we pray in a more interior manner over the course of the day, we will be surprised at noticing our breath and remembering God Trinity and who we are, in moments of work or after work, walking in nature, hearing the sounds of birds with new appreciation, and feeling the breeze or wind as cues of God's everywhereness. And then in quiet, following the Spirit's lead within, to the heart of who we are, leaving images and thoughts behind. Inward in committed communion.

Contemplative Reception of Artistic Expression

Artistic expression is a creative work in a wide range of media, as well as an opening of emotional space to find the artist and ourselves. Art can reveal what words cannot.

Visual expressions stand out in the great icons of the face of God in Christ the *pantocrator*, of his pancosmic presence to us. Both his humanity and divinity are so well expressed in the grand twelfth-century apsial mosaic in Monreale, Sicily, where Byzantine and Western traditions meet.

The Trinitarian icon of the Russian monk Andrei Rublev presents three angels seated at table, as Orthodox norms for the icon exclude representation of the Father or the Spirit; the open space at the table is meaningful: it is for our presence. Theologian Catherine Mowry LaCugna finds a circle that is not closed. "One has the distinct sensation when meditating on the icon that one is not only invited into this communion but, indeed, one already is part of it."[4] An icon is about experienced encounter and intends to evoke awareness of our spirit into the divine presence. A small, simple icon of the face of Christ invites us to encounter him who is living now and to rest in his gaze and eyes of love. Our first encounter with icons requires time for our reverent and silent openness.

St. Augustine said the person who sings prays twice. As noted, Leonardo Boff finds beauty in the ancient hymns to the Holy Spirit and their reliance of living faith on the Spirit with the repetition "come." The prayer to come is both the assurance of relationship and an appeal to the Spirit who dwells within to emerge for our often clouded awareness. Boff turns our attention to the faith expression of the hymns and not simply their performance.

The humanities can bring us to our humanity by our self-expression and receiving that of our contemporaries and those who've gone before us. Our humanity is that which is fundamentally open to God; we live in a supernatural existential. Rahner wrote that "artists are discoverers of a concrete situation in which persons discover their transcendental being in a new way...."[5] Writers, practitioners of the visual arts, and musicians can profoundly evoke the transcendental and religious in us.

Artistic expressions do not need religious themes to evoke the transcendent. Rahner writes: "If hearing is not the work of the ears alone, but of the whole person, an acoustical phenomenon—depending on the human context in which it takes place—may be religious or not."[6] In jazz music, saxophonist John Coltrane offers me an expressed Trinitarian analogy in a particular performance of his composition "*Naima.*" The drummer who begins, underlies, and closes the piece seems like the Father, source and goal. The two hands of the Father are evoked for me, both in Coltrane's saxophone, as if the Word comes forth in an intimate and perhaps lamenting presence to our lived condition; and emerging in the piano, the Spirit imaged, echoing the empathy of the saxophone, with a brightness of support and sustenance bringing energy, confidence, and joy. Trinity heard in music is more suggested and experiential, but with effect.[7]

The poetry and prayer of Judaism and Christianity appear in the Book of Psalms, expressing the stages, joys, and sorrows of life. A. Chouraqi wrote that "We were born with this book in our very bones."

Psalm 116 (117) is the shortest psalm and may be the one essential psalm to commit to heart and invoke in prayer from the heart to the cosmos. It is a universal invitation to praise God's essential and non-specified love:

> Alleluia.
> O praise the Lord, all you nations,
> acclaim him all you peoples!
> Strong is his love for us;
> he is faithful for ever.[8]

More Everydayness and Our Life Span

The music of the divine is woven into our everydayness. Breath remembrance can accompany spousal and familial encounters. An invited hug or embrace can open a new depth of encounter; I am bringing myself and available to you, expressed in open arms in the moment.

If, as in the Catholic tradition, marriage is a sacrament, then sexual encounters of all levels in marriage are holy and sacramental. Awareness of relationship helps the person to be encountered in marriage, family, and all relationships. Breath in God can truly bring us to the moment and make the difference by our self-disposal to the gifts of the Spirit, intended for this moment, so we can truly be ourselves for the encounter.

I recently suggested to a young mother with a reflective, joyous, and contemplative spirit that she practice the breath meditation in the Spirit and the Beloved as her baby rests on her. She later shared her practice and hope for an ongoing restful baby! Can't this be a perfect form of contemplative prayer, when parent and child find themselves one within the lifegiving love of God Trinity?

Prayer practice needs the preparation and study we have offered but is actually for simple lived awareness that we are in the Trinity's centrifugal and centripetal love at this moment. It can be treasured throughout life.

Affection in family life, including simple hugs with our children as teenagers and adults are manifestations of our spiritual life, too, when there are just and loving relationships among persons. We receive each other and respond to each other in the invited hug or embrace. And

I've found that a family dog who sits on my lap can bring me back to myself in God, as I find this small animal a link to the cosmos in peace. It's all in how we dispose ourselves.

Communion with God necessarily opens us to communion with our brothers and sisters and everything. God Trinity's centrifugal and centripetal loving is all encompassing. We love more deeply and experience the sadness and suffering and brokenness of the world more deeply, as the Spirit accompanies our love to our sisters and brothers.

We will experience our own brokenness as well. As we grow in the outward and inward movement of God, our gaps and failings might be painfully apparent but should not be the basis of losing hope for ourselves. These can be moments of self-recovery and self-remembering as for the Prodigal Son, and the first step to reconciliation and renewal as beloved.

Profoundly difficult moments will find us—sickness, the experience of abandonment, or facing death. Jesus lived both communion with the Father and anguish in his suffering.

Return to our breath is difficult in a health or other crisis. I have had some experience of anguish as well as the rest in relatedness with God. Relatedness was all I asked. If we can continue to breathe our reception and response to the breath, we can hope our relatedness of communion beneath everything would be somehow present again, for some rest and then courage for the next steps, perhaps as a beckoning to renewed health, or a continued lesser state or, finally, to reckoning with death.

Karl Rahner developed a theology of death that reasserts it as a human and not simply physical event. Very simply stated, death is both our final undoing as well as our consummation. The undoing may have progressed over years or decades, or arisen suddenly. Illness and death do not seem fitting for humanity as God's work of art. Yet consummation is present as well, the deeper meaning of death as completion of our trajectory of love in communion in God.[9]

In compline, the night prayer of the Western Church, there is the daily Scripture versicle, "Into your hands, O Lord, I commend my spirit." Giving ourselves over to God and St. Irenaeus' two hands of God can give this prayer great meaning. It prepares us for every day of life and death. Rahner wrote that he hoped to make this prayer in the face of death. Harshly disruptive as the transition of death is, communion, return, and consummation underlie it.

Last Words and a Memory of Blessed John

We began by affirming our identity and communion with God, and so it is fitting in our close. Relationship with God comes with being human. Relationship is created and revealed by God's Word and Breath and is fulfilled in God's self-bestowal to us, or grace, for union in this moment and in consummation, or glory. All persons and the very cosmos with its molecules of which we are made are enfolded in love.

Reception of our breath can be the entry point or recovery of our primal identity as Beloved of God. A contemplative life lives faith, hope, and love in Spirit; in the gifts of the Spirit, wisdom, understanding, counsel, knowledge, reverence, fortitude, and awe; and in the fruits of the Spirit, in love, joy, peace, patience, kindness, goodness, faithfulness, gentleness, and self-control.

As we look ahead, may our ongoing hearing and reading of Scripture and sacred doctrine surprise us with new understanding of the activity of the two hands of God, the pancosmic presence of Christ, and the omnipresent strong and gentle movement of the Spirit, the Breath of God.

May we breathe in God, following the Spirit Breath within, to ourselves and to an imageless communion in God Trinity.

Blessed John sends us on with his loving appreciation and remembrance of Jesus' Last Supper prayer for our experience of personal loving communion (John 17:21–23). Each of his words has meaning for our meditative love:

> That is what Christ desired when he prayed to his heavenly Father that all his beloved might be perfectly one, even as he is one with the Father in blissful enjoyment through the Holy Spirit. He thus prayed and desired that he might be one in us and we one in him and in his holy heavenly Father in blissful enjoyment through the Holy Spirit. I consider this the most loving prayer which Christ ever prayed for our salvation.[10]

Notes

1   Clement of Alexandria, *Clement of Alexandria: Exhortation to the Greeks, The Rich Man's Salvation, To the Newly Baptized,* Trans. G.W. Butterworth (Cambridge, MA; London: Harvard University Press, 1919, 2003), 213.

2   Karl Rahner, *Theological Investigations: Volume XXIII: Final Writings*, trans. Joseph Donceel, SJ, and Hugh M. Riley (New York: Crossroad, 1992), 203.

3   Rowan Williams, *Being Christian: Baptism, Bible, Eucharist, Prayer* (Grand Rapids, MI; Cambridge, UK: William B. Eerdmans Publishing Company, 2014), 61–62. Williams is a theologian with a particular devotion to early theology who served as the Archbishop of Canterbury. He shares the ancient tradition with contemporary persons and our needs so that theology will be properly practical.

4   Catherine Mowry LaCugna, "God in Communion with Us," in *Freeing Theology: The Essentials of Theology in Feminist Perspective*, ed. Catherine Mowry LaCugna (San Francisco: HarperCollins, 1993), 84. Trinity means radical inclusiveness and boundarylessness affirming "like Rublev's icon, that true communion among persons is the deepest meaning of life" (108).

5   Karl Rahner, "Art against the Horizon of Theology and Piety," in *Theological Investigations: Volume XXIII: Final Writings*, trans. Joseph Donceel, SJ, and Hugh M. Riley (New York: Crossroad, 1992), 166. He relies on the ancient *analogia entis*, by which all things can be seen as related and lead ultimately to God. In the same article (164), Rahner encourages theology to go beyond a rationalistic account. A next step, "although not new, has been neglected during the last few centuries: theology must somehow be 'mystagogical,' that is, should not merely speak about objects in abstract concepts, but it must encourage people really to experience that which is expressed in such concepts." I believe Rahner practiced an experiential theology. It is the spirit in which this study and practice is attempted.

6   Ibid, 166.

7   John Coltrane, "Naima," in *Giant Steps*, recorded in 1959. I reference "Naima" of the original album; a reissue has an alternate version as well, with a different pianist. (In the original, Wynton Kelly was on piano and Jimmy Cobb on drums.) "Naima" was performed regularly by Coltrane. *Blue World* (2019) is a CD with several takes of "Naima," with their own power. *Blue World* does have two tracks of "Village Blues" that have a Trinitarian evocation, and lead with the piano, suggesting to me the Spirit hovering in the early cosmos, with the synergy of the saxophone responding, as the two hands of the Father. Bass and drum suggest the ever presence of Father as inception, unifier, and goal.

8   *The Psalms: A New Translation from the Hebrew Arranged for Singing to the Psalmody of Joseph Gelineau* (New York and Mahwah, NJ: Paulist Press, 1968), 204.

9   Joseph Piccione, *Death and Consummation in Christ: A Theology of Care of the Sick and Dying in Light of the Thought of Karl Rahner, SJ* (unpublished dissertation, Baltimore, 2009).

10 Ruusbroec, "The Little Book of Clarification," in *John Ruusbroec: The Spiritual Espousals and Other Works*, 266.

www.ingramcontent.com/pod-product-compliance
Lightning Source LLC
Chambersburg PA
CBHW020950230426
43666CB00005B/253